Winning Lottery Lines

Winning Lottery Lines

by Harry Schneider

Strategic Book Publishing
New York, NewYork

Strategic Books Publishing
An imprint of AEG Publishing Group
845 Third Avenue, 6th Floor - 6016
New York, NY 10022
www.StrategicBookPublishing.com

ISBN: 978-1-60693-159-2
SKU: 1-60693-159-8

Printed in the United States of America

Book Design: Rolando F. Santos

Dedication

I dedicate this book to Thomas Charles Gregor Gledall,
our new charming little grandson who was born on March 5, 2008.

Contents

Preface

IT is said that any line of six random numbers stands exactly the same chance of being drawn in any lottery as any other line of six random numbers. The odds for any line of six numbers to be drawn in a forty-nine-numbered lottery is always 1 in 13, 983, 816.

Is this absolutely true? There are two ways that the lottery could be drawn: One way would be to have each of the 13,983,816 combinations written out on a strip of paper. The draw would simply be the random extraction of one strip of paper bearing six numbers. The other way is the present way of drawing each number separately by using numbered balls.

If the draw was made the first way, then, indeed, the odds of any combination is exactly the same as any other. There would be no value in any statistical analysis. However, when the numbers are drawn separately, then there is an opportunity to analyse and exploit the situation. Let me show you something.

Take 10, 20, 30, and 40. These numbers are known in mathematics as the base tens series. When the first ball is drawn in any lottery of forty-nine numbers, the odds of getting one of the tens is 4 in 49. If one of them is drawn, the odds of getting another is 3 in 48. Notice that the odds change. This is the point. Here we have a system where odds are meant to be the same and unchanging, but clearly we have a situation where we observe odds changing.

At this point don't worry if you have difficulty grasping this concept. You are in good company. While valuable use of statistical reasoning is made every day in many industries, there are a few professional mathematicians who state that, "because of the many anomalies in statistics, the concept of statistical reasoning is very unsound."

Take another example, which is a clincher!

There are 593,775 ways of arranging six numbers 1 through 30.

There are 13,983,816 ways of arranging six numbers 1 through 49.

This means that there should be a sequence out of 1 through 30 drawn approximately every twenty-four weeks (i.e. 13,983,816 divided by 593,775. This is 23.55).

However if every sequence shares the same odds, then why does this usually not happen? It does happen, in fact, but is very rare, only being recorded twice in five years. Therefore, in only 0.1 percent of the time since the beginning of all twentieth-century lotteries, have winning jackpot lines had their largest number being less than 30. This is incredible! Most mathematicians believe that every possible line has the same equal chance of being drawn. My research shows that instead of there being a 4.25 percent chance of numbers within the range of 1 through 30, there is only a 0.1 percent chance. This is nearly forty-three times fewer. Clearly this is not an "equality" situation.

There seems to be a situation here that we can exploit to our advantage. However, the main thrust of my argument for examining different sequences of numbers is the concept of entropy. The Oxford English Dictionary states entropy "...as a measure of the degree of disorder or randomness in the system...," which I interpret to mean, "out of order, chaos and randomness always ensues."

Take the following example of a small container with the bottom half filled with salt and the top half filled with pepper. This is an ordered situation. Now shake the container and it immediately changes to a grey amorphous mix. Shake it for as many million years as you wish and an ordered situation will never appear again.

This is the motive behind this book. From the ordered start position of the lottery balls, they are rarely drawn in an ordered sequence. It follows that if one identifies order in one's own selection, then you should seriously consider choosing a more random sequence.

As we progress through the book you will find other important logical instances demonstrated to your satisfaction. These we can exploit. Know, however, that it is not my intention to recommend what type of numbers to play. My recommendations consist of cautioning you on entering too many numbers of a certain type.

Acknowledgments

I would like to express my gratitude and thanks to the following people whose encouragement, help, and support made this book possible: Jacquie Schneider (to whom I am especially grateful), Barry Shepherd, Simon Donnelly, Steve South, and Gilles Dussault.

Last, but not least, I would like to pay tribute to Karl Friedrich Gauss (1777–1855) whose ideas I liberally purloined.

CHART 1

UK 2007 SATURDAY RESULTS
ANALYSIS OF LOTTERY NUMBERS DIVISIBLE BY 2

WEEK No.	LOTTERY NUMBERS DRAWN						TOTAL IN WEEK	NUMBER OF TIMES PER WEEK IN YEAR						
								0	1	2	3	4	5	6
1	15	25	29	35	39	40	1		X	X	X	X	X	
2	05	08	12	20	28	48	5		X	X	X	X	X	
3	04	07	26	28	39	49	3		X	X	X	X	X	
4	04	15	21	23	24	38	3		X	X	X	X	X	
5	13	17	39	46	47	49	1		X	X	X	X		
6	22	26	38	39	41	42	4		X	X	X	X		
7	06	18	40	43	47	49	3		X	X	X	X		
8	05	18	26	34	42	49	4			X	X	X		
9	01	05	11	19	28	36	2			X	X	X		
10	01	09	16	34	38	41	3			X	X	X		
11	01	09	14	20	43	44	3			X	X	X		
12	09	14	26	28	30	45	4				X	X		
13	03	35	39	42	44	48	3				X	X		
14	23	24	30	31	33	37	2				X			
15	13	16	23	29	36	49	2				X			
16	14	20	21	30	41	46	4				X			
17	11	17	24	28	41	47	2	0	7	11	16	13	4	0
18	04	33	34	38	39	49	3							
19	03	06	09	12	40	43	3							
20	17	19	20	32	36	48	4							
21	03	15	19	24	28	34	3							
22	01	10	33	35	38	43	2							
23	02	03	23	33	40	46	3							
24	08	17	33	41	43	45	1							
25	06	12	19	25	31	41	2							
26	10	11	17	34	38	46	4							
27	16	22	28	30	33	35	4							
28	15	27	35	37	38	39	1							
29	03	10	21	25	29	49	1							
30	04	18	22	27	44	48	5							
31	12	23	25	26	34	49	3							
32	06	10	11	19	22	46	4							
33	02	12	26	32	37	47	4							
34	07	13	17	33	40	42	2							
35	03	27	34	41	42	48	3							
36	04	10	20	24	39	49	4							
37	03	07	12	21	25	36	2							
38	03	12	15	18	30	31	3							
39	01	09	10	11	16	49	2							
40	05	06	18	22	24	38	5							
41	07	11	12	36	38	39	3							
42	04	15	25	27	33	40	2							
43	06	08	10	13	22	32	5							
44	03	10	22	25	31	49	1							
45	05	11	13	18	25	35	1							
46	11	16	20	22	27	46	4							
47	01	14	25	37	39	47	1							
48	12	24	33	36	39	42	4							
49	04	06	10	11	24	33	4							
50	12	22	25	43	46	49	3							
51	11	13	14	16	21	44	3							
52	04	13	23	28	30	32	4							

Chapter 1

The Odds and Evens of It

HAVE a look at Chart 1. In the first column under the word *week* are the numbers 1 through 52. These refer to the week numbers of the 2007 U.K. National Lottery, Saturday draw. The second set of numbers under the heading of *Lottery Numbers Drawn* refers to the numbers drawn in that week.

So, in week 1, the lottery numbers drawn were: 15, 25 29, 35, 39 and 40. In week 2, the numbers drawn were: 05, 08, 12, 20, 28, and 48. And so on…

You will see that some numbers on this part of the chart are highlighted in a square. (Note that all highlighting is done this way throughout this book.) These are even numbers, those exactly divisible by two.

In week 1, 40 was drawn. Being an even number, it is highlighted. In week 2, 05, 08, 12, 20, 28, and 48 were drawn. They are all highlighted as they are also even.

The third column is entitled *Total In Week*. This is where the total weekly number of even numbers is recorded. In this column against week 1, there is only one even number drawn, so "1" is placed in that column. In the same column against week 2, there are five even numbers drawn, so "5" is placed in that spot. And so on . . .

The right hand side of the chart shows Xs in boxes and forms a separate diagram. This diagram shows a picture of how the even numbers fell on a weekly basis over the year in question. For example, if you count how many times one even number occurred in the *Total* column, you will see that there were seven. So, therefore, there are seven Xs under the 1 column of this diagram. The number 7 is shown at the bottom of this diagram in the same column to indicate the total number of times an even number was drawn.

Also in the *Total* column you will count that there were eleven weeks where there were two even numbers drawn. So there are eleven Xs under the 2 column of this diagram. The number 11 is shown at the bottom of the diagram in the same column.

There were sixteen weeks in that year where there were three even numbers counted in the draw. And so on . . .

My main conclusion from looking at Chart 1 is that there were no weeks where the lottery numbers drawn were either all odd or all even. So, if you happen accidentally to have chosen six even numbers or six odd numbers as your lottery selection, you should consider choosing a fresh selection to take that fact into account.

In other words, make sure that you have 1, 2, 3, 4, or 5 even numbers in your selection. Applying this conclusion gives us a distinct advantage over our fellow punters. We must, however, check to make sure that the above conclusion is sound by checking it against the results of the first year of another lottery.

Have a look at Chart 2. It's made up in the same way as Chart 1, except that the lottery numbers shown are taken from the Canadian 2007 Lotto results. At first glance, these results look similar to the U.K. diagram. The Xs form an upside-down, bell-shaped curve. This curve has been shown in many lottery books and magazines and is called by mathematicians the "normal distribution" or "Gaussian curve." (Gauss was one of the first mathematicians who studied statistics.)

You will see that there was mainly between one and four even numbers drawn in most weeks of the U.K. National Lottery. But, more to the point, in the 2007 Canadian Lotto there was only one week where any of the six numbers drawn were all even. Also, there was only one week when there was a draw with five even numbers.

> **Statistically Challenged?**
>
> Don't panic! You don't have to understand statistics at all in order to benefit from this book. All you have to do is simply take notice of the conclusions written up in boldface italics at the end of each explanation.

Remember, in the 2007 U.K. Lottery, I concluded that you should never choose a selection of lottery numbers that are all odd or all even. This chart supports the assertion that your *future lottery selections should never be all odd or all even.*

CHART 2

2007 CANADIAN LOTTO RESULTS
ANALYSIS OF LOTTERY NUMBERS DIVISIBLE BY 2

WEEK No.	LOTTERY NUMBERS DRAWN						TOTAL IN WEEK	NUMBER OF TIMES PER WEEK IN YEAR						
								0	1	2	3	4	5	6
1	19	20	33	43	45	47	1	X	X	X	X	X	X	X
2	01	02	03	19	25	41	1	X	X	X	X	X		
3	24	40	45	47	48	49	2		X	X	X	X		
4	06	09	17	20	22	40	4		X	X	X	X		
5	10	13	24	27	37	39	2		X	X	X	X		
6	08	13	23	37	41	42	2		X	X	X	X		
7	13	20	31	36	43	46	3		X	X	X	X		
8	04	06	15	33	38	40	4		X	X	X			
9	03	21	27	37	43	44	1			X	X			
10	09	18	28	37	42	49	3			X	X			
11	13	21	23	27	28	34	2			X	X			
12	01	13	19	26	32	46	3			X	X			
13	04	09	16	32	37	41	3			X	X			
14	10	12	23	26	35	37	3				X			
15	06	15	22	26	41	49	3				X			
16	17	29	33	43	45	49	0				X			
17	03	19	20	23	35	38	2				X			
18	01	23	26	28	33	40	3				X			
19	05	07	13	27	45	47	0				X			
20	08	16	33	37	40	42	4				X			
21	06	17	29	32	36	47	3	2	8	13	20	7	1	1
22	08	16	19	32	40	46	5							
23	10	20	25	41	44	46	4							
24	03	15	31	33	43	48	1							
25	07	20	24	37	43	49	2							
26	06	12	25	43	45	47	2							
27	10	19	25	31	37	40	2							
28	10	27	33	38	40	49	3							
29	09	10	22	29	38	41	3							
30	01	05	17	32	39	45	1							
31	09	17	18	20	41	49	2							
32	01	17	23	34	37	49	1							
33	02	12	32	34	38	48	5							
34	09	19	31	35	39	42	1							
35	11	17	18	28	31	46	3							
36	03	08	16	20	24	25	4							
37	09	39	40	43	46	48	3							
38	05	08	12	15	39	47	2							
39	09	19	26	29	39	45	1							
40	05	15	30	35	41	48	2							
41	01	26	30	32	39	47	3							
42	07	08	13	26	32	35	3							
43	12	13	17	34	40	47	3							
44	08	23	33	40	46	49	3							
45	03	13	14	17	20	42	3							
46	14	17	27	41	47	48	2							
47	01	10	25	27	30	36	3							
48	16	21	31	40	43	45	2							
49	02	09	11	22	35	45	2							
50	03	11	32	34	44	48	4							
51	08	17	30	36	40	47	4							
52	07	13	16	24	35	42	3							

CHART 3

UK 2007 SATURDAY RESULTS
ANALYSIS OF LOTTERY NUMBERS DIVISIBLE BY 3.

WEEK No.	LOTTERY NUMBERS DRAWN						TOTAL IN WEEK	NUMBER OF TIMES PER WEEK IN YEAR						
								0	1	2	3	4	5	6
1	15	25	29	35	39	40	2	X	X	X	X	X	X	X
2	05	08	12	20	28	48	2		X	X	X	X		
3	04	07	26	28	39	49	1		X	X	X	X		
4	04	15	21	23	24	38	3		X	X	X	X		
5	13	17	39	46	47	49	1		X	X	X			
6	22	26	38	39	41	42	2		X	X	X			
7	06	18	40	43	47	49	2		X	X	X			
8	05	18	26	34	42	49	2		X	X	X			
9	01	05	11	19	28	36	1		X	X	X			
10	01	09	16	34	38	41	1		X	X	X			
11	01	09	14	20	43	44	1		X	X				
12	09	14	26	28	30	45	3		X	X				
13	03	35	39	42	44	48	4		X	X				
14	23	24	30	31	33	37	3		X	X				
15	13	16	23	29	36	49	1		X	X				
16	14	20	21	30	41	46	2		X					
17	11	17	24	28	41	47	1		X					
18	04	33	34	38	39	49	2		X					
19	03	06	09	12	40	43	4		X					
20	17	19	20	32	36	48	2		X					
21	03	15	19	24	28	34	3	1	20	15	10	4	1	1
22	01	10	33	35	38	43	1							
23	02	03	23	33	40	46	2							
24	08	17	33	41	43	45	2							
25	06	12	19	25	31	41	2							
26	10	11	17	34	38	46	0							
27	16	22	28	30	33	35	2							
28	15	27	35	37	38	39	3							
29	03	10	21	25	29	49	2							
30	04	18	22	27	44	48	3							
31	12	23	25	26	34	49	1							
32	06	10	11	19	22	46	1							
33	02	12	26	32	37	47	1							
34	07	13	17	33	40	42	2							
35	03	27	34	41	42	48	4							
36	04	10	20	24	39	49	2							
37	03	07	12	21	25	36	4							
38	03	12	15	18	30	31	5							
39	01	09	10	11	16	49	1							
40	05	06	18	22	24	38	3							
41	07	11	12	36	38	39	3							
42	04	15	25	27	33	40	3							
43	06	08	10	13	22	32	1							
44	03	10	22	25	31	49	1							
45	05	11	13	18	25	35	1							
46	11	16	20	22	27	46	1							
47	01	14	25	37	39	47	1							
48	12	24	33	36	39	42	6							
49	04	06	10	11	24	33	3							
50	12	22	25	43	46	49	1							
51	11	13	14	16	21	44	1							
52	04	13	23	28	30	32	1							

4

Chapter 2

Considering Numbers Divisible by 3

NOW let's take a look at Chart 3 *(opposite)*. It's exactly the same basic results of the U.K. 2007 Lottery results shown in Chart 1. This time, the analysis is based on finding out which numbers divide exactly by three. Theory indicates that as there are about one third of the numbers exactly divisible by 3, then about one third of the drawn numbers should be expected to be exactly divisible by 3.

In the fifty-two weeks of 2007, there were 312 main lottery numbers drawn. About one third of them, 104 of them to be exact, should have been exactly divisible by 3. The actual total drawn that were exactly divisible by 3 was 103. This is very close, and just shows that the law of averages indicating that there are an average of two numbers exactly divisible by 3 drawn each week is confirmed. These are solid facts! You can either take notice of them or ignore them at your own risk!

> **Just the Six**
>
> For the sake of simplifying matters I am excluding the bonus number and am only considering the choosing of the six "regular" numbers.

The first bit of advice indicated is that you should try to have at least two of your lottery selections being exactly divisible by 3. Looking at Chart 3, you will see that there were fifteen weeks where there were two numbers drawn that were exactly divisible by 3. This is most of the year!

Consider this: Twenty weeks out of the year, there was one number drawn that was exactly divisible by 3; for fifteen weeks out of the year, two of the numbers drawn were exactly divisible by 3; and for ten weeks out of the year, three numbers exactly divisible by 3 were drawn.

However, in my opinion, the most important thing to note is that there were hardly any weeks at all where five or six of the weekly numbers drawn were exactly divisible by 3. This leads us to the second and most important piece of advice: *Consider not having more than four numbers in your lottery picks on any given week be divisible by 3.* For example, a line consisting of: 3, 9, 12, 24, 36, and 48 is a definite no-no, as all six of these selections are exactly divisible by 3. A line consisting of: 6, 18, 21, 27, 42, and 43 is also not a very good choice because there are five numbers present that are exactly divisible by 3. An acceptable line following this conclusion might be: 3, 4, 17, 22, 39, and 44, as only two of the numbers (3 and 39) are exactly divisible by 3.

But before you blindly accept the above advice as fact, you should examine Chart 4 to see if it confirms our suspicions. If it does, then perhaps we can adopt yet another valuable policy to help us in our quest of securing a lottery win!

Have a look at Chart 4, back again with the 2007 Canadian Lotto results of that year. This time I have analysed them by dividing each of the numbers drawn, excluding bonus numbers, by 3. We can directly compare Chart 4 with Chart 3.

The curve that encompasses the Xs is roughly the same in Chart 4 as that in Chart 3. But, the most important comparison is that there was never a week in the 2007 Canadian Lotto where all six, or even five, of the numbers were exactly divisible by 3. Had we taken notice of the advice indicated by the U.K. Lottery, we would have been spot on!

While we know not to have six or even five of our lottery picks be exactly divisible by 3, you might decide to be sure that there are not even four of your selected numbers divisible exactly by 3. However, you must remember that there is still a slight possibility that four of the drawn numbers could be evenly divisible by 3. After all, there was one week where there was indeed a line with four numbers evenly divisible by 3. But, you might quite safely ignore that.

To remind you precisely what I'm doing here let us reiterate our strategy: I am looking at 2007 U.K. Lottery results and examining them with various types of analysis and comparing the same type of analysis with the 2007 Canadian Lotto results. If the comparison is the same, I adopt a policy to take advantage of this. This then helps us to choose our future lottery selections wisely.

CHART 4

CANADIAN LOTTO RESULTS
ANALYSIS OF LOTTERY NUMBERS DIVISIBLE BY 3.

WEEK No.	LOTTERY NUMBERS DRAWN						TOTAL IN WEEK	NUMBER OF TIMES PER WEEK IN YEAR						
								0	1	2	3	4	5	6
1	19	20	[33]	43	[45]	47	2	X	X	X	X	X		
2	01	02	[03]	19	25	41	1	X	X	X	X			
3	[24]	40	[45]	47	[48]	49	3	X	X	X	X			
4	[06]	[09]	17	20	22	40	2	X	X	X	X			
5	10	13	[24]	[27]	37	[39]	3	X	X	X	X			
6	08	13	23	37	41	[42]	1	X	X	X	X			
7	13	20	31	[36]	43	46	1		X	X	X			
8	04	[06]	[15]	[33]	38	40	3		X	X	X			
9	[03]	[21]	[27]	37	43	44	3		X	X	X			
10	[09]	[18]	28	37	[42]	49	3		X	X	X			
11	13	[21]	23	[27]	28	34	2		X	X	X			
12	01	13	19	26	32	46	0		X	X	X			
13	04	[09]	16	32	37	41	1			X				
14	10	[12]	23	26	35	37	1			X				
15	[06]	[15]	22	26	41	49	2			X				
16	17	29	[33]	43	[45]	49	2			X				
17	[03]	19	20	23	35	38	1			X				
18	01	23	26	28	[33]	40	1			X				
19	05	07	13	[27]	[45]	47	2			X				
20	08	16	[33]	37	40	[42]	2			X				
21	[06]	17	29	32	[36]	47	2			X				
22	08	16	19	32	40	46	0	6	12	21	12	1	0	0
23	10	20	25	41	44	46	0							
24	[03]	[15]	31	[33]	43	[48]	4							
25	07	20	[24]	37	43	49	1							
26	[06]	[12]	25	43	[45]	47	3							
27	10	19	25	31	37	40	0							
28	10	[27]	[33]	38	40	49	2							
29	[09]	10	22	29	38	41	1							
30	01	05	17	32	[39]	[45]	2							
31	[09]	17	[18]	20	41	49	2							
32	01	17	23	34	37	49	0							
33	02	[12]	32	34	38	[48]	2							
34	[09]	19	31	35	[39]	[42]	3							
35	11	17	[18]	28	31	46	1							
36	[03]	08	16	20	[24]	25	2							
37	[09]	[39]	40	43	46	[48]	3							
38	05	08	[12]	[15]	[39]	47	3							
39	[09]	19	26	29	[39]	[45]	3							
40	05	[15]	[30]	35	41	[48]	3							
41	01	26	[30]	32	[39]	47	2							
42	07	08	13	26	32	35	0							
43	[12]	13	17	34	40	47	1							
44	08	23	[33]	40	46	49	1							
45	[03]	13	14	17	20	[42]	2							
46	14	17	[27]	41	47	[48]	2							
47	01	10	25	[27]	[30]	[36]	3							
48	16	[21]	31	40	43	[45]	2							
49	02	[09]	11	22	35	[45]	2							
50	[03]	11	32	34	44	[48]	2							
51	08	17	[30]	[36]	40	47	2							
52	07	13	16	[24]	35	[42]	2							

Make no mistake, though, I have not yet cracked a certain way of winning—I am discovering why people lose so often. Then, by avoiding errors in our selections, we stand a much better chance of obtaining a winning line.

Lottery companies know that we should get some sort of a win in the region of once every fifty-four tries. By using the methods shown in this book, I have easily accomplished the odds of a win in the region of at least once in every thirty-six tries on average. Hopefully you, too, will soon be accomplishing this amazing improvement. I have made many inquiries to lottery participants and some never achieve a win of any sort, even once in fifty-four tries.

Chapter 3

Those Divisible by 4

OKAY, on to Chart 5 *(next page)*. Yes, it's the same set of lottery numbers we saw in Charts 1 and 3. This time, we have highlighted the numbers that are exactly divisible by 4. The weekly totals are added and shown in the right-hand column as Xs, just as in previous charts.

How many lottery numbers in this draw would you expect to be exactly divisible by 4? Well, there are six main numbers drawn every week. There are fifty-two weeks in the year. This makes six times fifty-two, which equals 312 numbers drawn in the year. Statistically, there should be about one-quarter of them exactly divisible by 4. So, you would expect to have about seventy-eight in the year. In fact, there were seventy-two. Close! Not too bad! This proves that the correct interpretation of the law of averages is still holding its own and that we are still absolutely correct in our approach!

Looking closely at Chart 5, it would seem to show that it might be to our advantage to have less than three numbers in any one line of our future selections be exactly divisible by 4. But, actually that is not the advice to which I am leading.

The most valuable observation is the fact that there was never a week where the numbers drawn were all exactly divisible by 4. Also, there was a single week where four and five of the numbers drawn were exactly divisible by 4. You might decide that you can ignore that occasion. In fact, it might seem better to have no numbers divisible by 4 in your selections. By now you must surely be coming to the inescapable conclusion that the numbers are trying to tell us something! Take notice of these facts or

Harry Schneider

CHART 5

UK 2007 SATURDAY RESULTS
ANALYSIS OF LOTTERY NUMBERS DIVISIBLE BY 4

WEEK No.	LOTTERY NUMBERS DRAWN						TOTAL IN WEEK	NUMBER OF TIMES PER WEEK IN YEAR						
								0	1	2	3	4	5	6
1	15	25	29	35	39	40	1	X	X	X	X	X	X	
2	05	08	12	20	28	48	5	X	X	X	X			
3	04	07	26	28	39	49	1	X	X	X	X			
4	04	15	21	23	24	38	2	X	X	X	X			
5	13	17	39	46	47	49	0	X	X	X				
6	22	26	38	39	41	42	0	X	X	X				
7	06	18	40	43	47	49	1	X	X	X				
8	05	18	26	34	42	49	0	X	X	X				
9	01	05	11	19	28	36	2	X	X	X				
10	01	09	16	34	38	41	1	X	X	X				
11	01	09	14	20	43	44	2	X	X	X				
12	09	14	26	28	30	45	1		X	X				
13	03	35	39	42	44	48	2		X	X				
14	23	24	30	31	33	37	1		X	X				
15	13	16	23	29	36	49	1		X	X				
16	14	20	21	30	41	46	1		X	X				
17	11	17	24	28	41	47	2		X					
18	04	33	34	38	39	49	1		X					
19	03	06	09	12	40	43	2		X					
20	17	19	20	32	36	48	4		X					
21	03	15	19	24	28	34	2	11	19	16	4	1	1	0
22	01	10	33	35	38	43	0							
23	02	03	23	33	40	46	2							
24	08	17	33	41	43	45	1							
25	06	12	19	25	31	41	1							
26	10	11	17	34	38	46	0							
27	16	22	28	30	33	35	2							
28	15	27	35	37	38	39	0							
29	03	10	21	25	29	49	0							
30	04	18	22	27	44	48	3							
31	12	23	25	26	34	49	1							
32	06	10	11	19	22	46	0							
33	02	12	26	32	37	47	2							
34	07	13	17	33	40	42	1							
35	03	27	34	41	42	48	1							
36	04	10	20	24	39	49	3							
37	03	07	12	21	25	36	2							
38	03	12	15	18	30	31	1							
39	01	09	10	11	16	49	1							
40	05	06	18	22	24	38	1							
41	07	11	12	36	38	39	2							
42	04	15	25	27	33	40	2							
43	06	08	10	13	22	32	2							
44	03	10	22	25	31	49	0							
45	05	11	13	18	25	35	0							
46	11	16	20	22	27	46	1							
47	01	14	25	37	39	47	0							
48	12	24	33	36	39	42	3							
49	04	06	10	11	24	33	2							
50	12	22	25	43	46	49	1							
51	11	13	14	16	21	44	2							
52	04	13	23	28	30	32	3							

10

CHART 6

CANADIAN LOTTO RESULTS 2007
ANALYSIS OF LOTTERY NUMBERS DIVISIBLE BY 4

WEEK No.	LOTTERY NUMBERS DRAWN						TOTAL IN WEEK	NUMBER OF TIMES PER WEEK IN YEAR						
								0	1	2	3	4	5	6
1	19	20	33	43	45	47	1	X	X	X	X	X		
2	01	02	03	19	25	41	0	X	X	X	X	X		
3	24	40	45	47	48	49	3	X	X	X	X			
4	06	09	17	20	22	40	2	X	X	X	X			
5	10	13	24	27	37	39	1	X	X	X	X			
6	08	13	23	37	41	42	1	X	X	X	X			
7	13	20	31	36	43	46	2	X	X	X				
8	04	06	15	33	38	40	2	X	X	X				
9	03	21	27	37	43	44	1	X	X	X				
10	09	18	28	37	42	49	1		X	X				
11	13	21	23	27	28	34	1		X	X				
12	01	13	19	26	32	46	1		X	X				
13	04	09	16	32	37	41	3		X	X				
14	10	12	23	26	35	37	1		X	X				
15	06	15	22	26	41	49	0		X					
16	17	29	33	43	45	49	0		X					
17	03	19	20	23	35	38	1		X					
18	01	23	26	28	33	40	2		X					
19	05	07	13	27	45	47	0		X					
20	08	16	33	37	40	42	3		X					
21	06	17	29	32	36	47	2		X					
22	08	16	19	32	40	46	4	9	21	14	6	2	0	0
23	10	20	25	41	44	46	2							
24	03	15	31	33	43	48	1							
25	07	20	24	37	43	49	2							
26	06	12	25	43	45	47	1							
27	10	19	25	31	37	40	1							
28	10	27	33	38	40	49	1							
29	09	10	22	29	38	41	0							
30	01	05	17	32	39	45	1							
31	09	17	18	20	41	49	1							
32	01	17	23	34	37	49	0							
33	02	12	32	34	38	48	3							
34	09	19	31	35	39	42	0							
35	11	17	18	28	31	46	1							
36	03	08	16	20	24	25	4							
37	09	39	40	43	46	48	2							
38	05	08	12	15	39	47	2							
39	09	19	26	29	39	45	0							
40	05	15	30	35	41	48	1							
41	01	26	30	32	39	47	1							
42	07	08	13	26	32	35	2							
43	12	13	17	34	40	47	2							
44	08	23	33	40	46	49	2							
45	03	13	14	17	20	42	1							
46	14	17	27	41	47	48	1							
47	01	10	25	27	30	36	1							
48	16	21	31	40	43	45	2							
49	02	09	11	22	35	45	0							
50	03	11	32	34	44	48	3							
51	08	17	30	36	40	47	3							
52	07	13	16	24	35	42	2							

11

ignore them if you dare! You can see that we have actually shown (if not proven) that it would be foolish to have four or more of your future lottery numbers be exactly divisible by 4.

So, our policy should be, ***when choosing a line of future lottery numbers, be sure that not more than four of them are divisibly by 4.***

Now, it just behoves us to check the chart of the 2007 Canadian Lotto numbers, Chart 6 *(previous page)*, to see if we would have been 100-percent correct had we actually taken the above advice. This time I have analysed the results of that year by looking at numbers exactly divisible by 4 in order to compare them with the analysis shown in Chart 5. The comparison bears out our advice: in no week of that year were there five or six numbers drawn that are exactly divisible by 4!

This must surely be confirmation that we are on the correct path to a winning formula. Logically, one would expect those years' results to have about seventy-eight of the numbers be exactly divisible by 4 (6 x 52/4). Count them up; there were, in fact, seventy-five. Yes, our use of the law of averages is still working very well!

Chapter 4

Those Divisible by 5

MOVING on to Chart 7 now *(next page)*, which is, of course, 2007 U.K. Lottery results once again. This time we're looking at the number of times the numbers are exactly divisible by 5 in the draw. I hope that the basic idea behind this book is getting clearer. Looking deeper into Chart 7, you will find that there were forty weeks where there was at least one of the results exactly divisible by 5. As this is more than three-quarters of the year, you might consider placing a number that is exactly divisible by 5 in most lines of your selections. But, as there were sixteen weeks in the year where there were no numbers exactly divisible by 5, then you will need to consider whether it is worth your doing so! While this is not entirely satisfactory, you may consider choosing at least one number that is divisible by 5 in your selection.

However, I do have a solid piece of advice to impart. Considering that there were no weeks in these results where there were five or six numbers drawn that were exactly divisible by 5. So, once again we are drawn to another policy that we should seriously consider: *When choosing a line of future lottery numbers ensure that five or six of them are not exactly divisible 5.*

Before we accept this policy, however, we should check to see if the 2007 Canadian lotto results in Chart 8 support our conclusion.

Chart 8 *(next page)* shows the Canadian Lotto results again and only one question needs to be asked here: "If we had taken the preceding advice, how would we have fared?" Our previous advice was to ensure that

Harry Schneider

CHART 7

UK 2007 SATURDAY RESULTS
ANALYSIS OF LOTTERY NUMBERS DIVISIBLE BY 5

WEEK No.	LOTTERY NUMBERS DRAWN						TOTAL IN WEEK	NUMBER OF TIMES PER WEEK IN YEAR						
								0	1	2	3	4	5	6
1	15	25	29	35	39	40	4	X	X	X	X	X		
2	05	08	12	20	28	48	2	X	X	X	X			
3	04	07	26	28	39	49	0	X	X	X				
4	04	15	21	23	24	38	1	X	X	X				
5	13	17	39	46	47	49	0	X	X	X				
6	22	26	38	39	41	42	0	X	X	X				
7	06	18	40	43	47	49	1	X	X	X				
8	05	18	26	34	42	49	1	X	X	X				
9	01	05	11	19	28	36	1	X	X	X				
10	01	09	16	34	38	41	0	X	X	X				
11	01	09	14	20	43	44	1	X	X					
12	09	14	26	28	30	45	2	X	X					
13	03	35	39	42	44	48	1		X					
14	23	24	30	31	33	37	1		X					
15	13	16	23	29	36	49	0		X					
16	14	20	21	30	41	46	2		X					
17	11	17	24	28	41	47	0		X					
18	04	33	34	38	39	49	0		X					
19	03	06	09	12	40	43	1		X					
20	17	19	20	32	36	48	1		X					
21	03	15	19	24	28	34	1		X					
22	01	10	33	35	38	43	2		X					
23	02	03	23	33	40	46	1		X					
24	08	17	33	41	43	45	1		X					
25	06	12	19	25	31	41	1		X					
26	10	11	17	34	38	46	1		X					
27	16	22	28	30	33	35	2		X					
28	15	27	35	37	38	39	2	12	27	10	2	1	0	0
29	03	10	21	25	29	49	2							
30	04	18	22	27	44	48	0							
31	12	23	25	26	34	49	1							
32	06	10	11	19	22	46	1							
33	02	12	26	32	37	47	0							
34	07	13	17	33	40	42	1							
35	03	27	34	41	42	48	0							
36	04	10	20	24	39	49	2							
37	03	07	12	21	25	36	1							
38	03	12	15	18	30	31	2							
39	01	09	10	11	16	49	1							
40	05	06	18	22	24	38	1							
41	07	11	12	36	38	39	0							
42	04	15	25	27	33	40	3							
43	06	08	10	13	22	32	1							
44	03	10	22	25	31	49	2							
45	05	11	13	18	25	35	3							
46	11	16	20	22	27	46	1							
47	01	14	25	37	39	47	1							
48	12	24	33	36	39	42	1							
49	04	06	10	11	24	33	1							
50	12	22	25	43	46	49	1							
51	11	13	14	16	21	44	0							
52	04	13	23	28	30	32	1							

14

CHART 8

CANADIAN LOTTO RESULTS 2007
ANALYSIS OF LOTTERY NUMBERS DIVISIBLE BY 5

WEEK No.	LOTTERY NUMBERS DRAWN						TOTAL IN WEEK	NUMBER OF TIMES PER WEEK IN YEAR						
								0	1	2	3	4	5	6
1	19	20	33	43	45	47	2	X	X	X	X			
2	01	02	03	19	25	41	1	X	X	X	X			
3	24	40	45	47	48	49	2	X	X	X	X			
4	06	09	17	20	22	40	2	X	X	X	X			
5	10	13	24	27	37	39	1	X	X	X				
6	08	13	23	37	41	42	0	X	X	X				
7	13	20	31	36	43	46	1	X	X	X				
8	04	06	15	33	38	40	2	X	X	X				
9	03	21	27	37	43	44	0	X	X	X				
10	09	18	28	37	42	49	0	X	X	X				
11	13	21	23	27	28	34	0	X	X	X				
12	01	13	19	26	32	46	0	X	X	X				
13	04	09	16	32	37	41	0		X	X				
14	10	12	23	26	35	37	2		X					
15	06	15	22	26	41	49	1		X					
16	17	29	33	43	45	49	1		X					
17	03	19	20	23	35	38	1		X					
18	01	23	26	28	33	40	1		X					
19	05	07	13	27	45	47	1		X					
20	08	16	33	37	40	42	1		X					
21	06	17	29	32	36	47	0		X					
22	08	16	19	32	40	46	1		X					
23	10	20	25	41	44	46	3		X					
24	03	15	31	33	43	48	1	12	23	13	4	0	0	0
25	07	20	24	37	43	49	1							
26	06	12	25	43	45	47	2							
27	10	19	25	31	37	40	3							
28	10	27	33	38	40	49	2							
29	09	10	22	29	38	41	1							
30	01	05	17	32	39	45	2							
31	09	17	18	20	41	49	1							
32	01	17	23	34	37	49	0							
33	02	12	32	34	38	48	0							
34	09	19	31	35	39	42	1							
35	11	17	18	28	31	46	0							
36	03	08	16	20	24	25	2							
37	09	39	40	43	46	48	1							
38	05	08	12	15	39	47	2							
39	09	19	26	29	39	45	1							
40	05	15	30	35	41	48	3							
41	01	26	30	32	39	47	1							
42	07	08	13	26	32	35	1							
43	12	13	17	34	40	47	1							
44	08	23	33	40	46	49	1							
45	03	13	14	17	20	42	1							
46	14	17	27	41	47	48	0							
47	01	10	25	27	30	36	3							
48	16	21	31	40	43	45	2							
49	02	09	11	22	35	45	2							
50	03	11	32	34	44	48	0							
51	08	17	30	36	40	47	2							
52	07	13	16	24	35	42	1							

15

five or six of our lottery picks are not exactly divisible by 5. Notice that the totals in columns 5 and 6 of Chart 8 are bare. We would have been absolutely, 100-percent correct. So, the advice is really sound! There are not even any lines with four numbers divisible by 4 present. This makes it quite safe to assume that there will be no instances where there are five or six numbers divisible by 5 present.

As with the previous charts, you might wish read a little further into it. There is an indication that you should, in fact, ensure that you have at least one of your future selections be exactly divisible by 5. But this advice is by no means 100-percent sound, as there were twelve weeks where there were no picks divisible by 5 at all.

In Chart 8 you can see that there were forty weeks in the year where there was at least one number present exactly divisible by 5. So, it seems that there may be something to gain by including one. However, as there was never a week with five or six numbers divisible by 5 in the draw, then the best conclusion must be: ***When choosing a line of future lottery numbers ensure that five or six of them are not exactly divisible by 5.***

Moving on to Chart 9, which showcases the same results from the 2007 U.K. lottery as before. This time, I have highlighted the numbers that were exactly divisible by 6. I then totalled up these highlighted numbers as before and entered the totals and Xs on the right-hand-side of the chart.

You'll notice that out of the picks on thirty-four weeks in that year, at least one of the numbers picked each week was exactly divisible by 6. But never was there a week where there were five or six of the draw numbers exactly divisible by 6. There happened to be a week where there were four numbers drawn that were divisible by 6, but even so, I would hesitate to choose a line with four numbers that were multiples of 6.

Remember this is a 100-percent result. So, 100 percent confidence, I can suggest another fruitful proposal. (You can probably guess by now what it will be.) ***When choosing a line of future lottery numbers, ensure that four, five, or six of them are not exactly divisible by 6.***

There are as many numbers exactly divisible by 6 as compared to lower numbers. The numbers exactly divisible by 6 are 6, 12, 18, 24, 30, 36, 42, and 48. Choosing a line of numbers such as 1, 6, 24, 30, 42, and 48 would be a dead loss, as there are five of the numbers exactly divisible by 6. Likewise, 4, 12, 18, 36, 42, and 48 would also be a dead loss, as there are also five numbers in the selection exactly divisible by 6. Another reason why it would be a bad choice is that they are also all even. You will remember in the first chapter, we concluded that it would be very unwise to have all your future selections be all even or all odd.

CHART 9

UK 2007 SATURDAY RESULTS
ANALYSIS OF LOTTERY NUMBERS DIVISIBLE BY 6

WEEK No.	LOTTERY NUMBERS DRAWN						TOTAL IN WEEK	NUMBER OF TIMES PER WEEK IN YEAR						
								0	1	2	3	4	5	6
1	15	25	29	35	39	40	0	X	X	X	X	X		
2	05	08	12	20	28	48	2	X	X	X	X			
3	04	07	26	28	39	49	0	X	X	X				
4	04	15	21	23	24	38	1	X	X	X				
5	13	17	39	46	47	49	0	X	X	X				
6	22	26	38	39	41	42	1	X	X	X				
7	06	18	40	43	47	49	2	X	X	X				
8	05	18	26	34	42	49	2	X	X	X				
9	01	05	11	19	28	36	1	X	X	X				
10	01	09	16	34	38	41	0	X	X	X				
11	01	09	14	20	43	44	0	X	X	X				
12	09	14	26	28	30	45	1	X	X	X				
13	03	35	39	42	44	48	2	X	X	X				
14	23	24	30	31	33	37	2	X	X	X				
15	13	16	23	29	36	49	1	X	X					
16	14	20	21	30	41	46	1	X	X					
17	11	17	24	28	41	47	1	X	X					
18	04	33	34	38	39	49	0	X	X					
19	03	06	09	12	40	43	2	18	18	13	2	1	0	0
20	17	19	20	32	36	48	2							
21	03	15	19	24	28	34	1							
22	01	10	33	35	38	43	0							
23	02	03	23	33	40	46	0							
24	08	17	33	41	43	45	0							
25	06	12	19	25	31	41	2							
26	10	11	17	34	38	46	0							
27	16	22	28	30	33	35	1							
28	15	27	35	37	38	39	0							
29	03	10	21	25	29	49	0							
30	04	18	22	27	44	48	2							
31	12	23	25	26	34	49	0							
32	06	10	11	19	22	46	1							
33	02	12	26	32	37	47	1							
34	07	13	17	33	40	42	1							
35	03	27	34	41	42	48	2							
36	04	10	20	24	39	49	1							
37	03	07	12	21	25	36	2							
38	03	12	15	18	30	31	3							
39	01	09	10	11	16	49	0							
40	05	06	18	22	24	38	3							
41	07	11	12	36	38	39	2							
42	04	15	25	27	33	40	0							
43	06	08	10	13	22	32	1							
44	03	10	22	25	31	49	0							
45	05	11	13	18	25	35	1							
46	11	16	20	22	27	46	0							
47	01	14	25	37	39	47	0							
48	12	24	33	36	39	42	4							
49	04	06	10	11	24	33	2							
50	12	22	25	43	46	49	1							
51	11	13	14	16	21	44	0							
52	04	13	23	28	30	32	1							

CHART 10

CANADIAN LOTTO RESULTS 2007
ANALYSIS OF LOTTERY NUMBERS DIVISIBLE BY 6

WEEK No.	LOTTERY NUMBERS DRAWN						TOTAL IN WEEK	NUMBER OF TIMES PER WEEK IN YEAR						
								0	1	2	3	4	5	6
1	19	20	33	43	45	47	0	X	X	X				
2	01	02	03	19	25	41	0	X	X	X				
3	24	40	45	47	48	49	2	X	X	X				
4	06	09	17	20	22	40	1	X	X	X				
5	10	13	24	27	37	39	1	X	X	X				
6	08	13	23	37	41	42	1	X	X	X				
7	13	20	31	36	43	46	1	X	X	X				
8	04	06	15	33	38	40	1	X	X	X				
9	03	21	27	37	43	44	0	X	X					
10	09	18	28	37	42	49	2	X	X					
11	13	21	23	27	28	34	0	X	X					
12	01	13	19	26	32	46	0	X	X					
13	04	09	16	32	37	41	0	X	X					
14	10	12	23	26	35	37	1	X	X					
15	06	15	22	26	41	49	1	X	X					
16	17	29	33	43	45	49	0	X	X					
17	03	19	20	23	35	38	0	X	X					
18	01	23	26	28	33	40	0	X	X					
19	05	07	13	27	45	47	0	X	X					
20	08	16	33	37	40	42	1	X	X					
21	06	17	29	32	36	47	2	X	X					
22	08	16	19	32	40	46	0	X						
23	10	20	25	41	44	46	0	22	21	9	0	0	0	0
24	03	15	31	33	43	48	1							
25	07	20	24	37	43	49	1							
26	06	12	25	43	45	47	2							
27	10	19	25	31	37	40	0							
28	10	27	33	38	40	49	0							
29	09	10	22	29	38	41	0							
30	01	05	17	32	39	45	0							
31	09	17	18	20	41	49	1							
32	01	17	23	34	37	49	0							
33	02	12	32	34	38	48	2							
34	09	19	31	35	39	42	1							
35	11	17	18	28	31	46	1							
36	03	08	16	20	24	25	1							
37	09	39	40	43	46	48	1							
38	05	08	12	15	39	47	1							
39	09	19	26	29	39	45	0							
40	05	15	30	35	41	48	2							
41	01	26	30	32	39	47	1							
42	07	08	13	26	32	35	0							
43	12	13	17	34	40	47	1							
44	08	23	33	40	46	49	0							
45	03	13	14	17	20	42	1							
46	14	17	27	41	47	48	1							
47	01	10	25	27	30	36	2							
48	16	21	31	40	43	45	0							
49	02	09	11	22	35	45	0							
50	03	11	32	34	44	48	1							
51	08	17	30	36	40	47	2							
52	07	13	16	24	35	42	2							

I can not say with absolute 100-percent certainty that you will never get a lottery result with four or more numbers exactly divisible by 6, but going on the above conclusion I would never choose a line where there are four or more numbers exactly divisible by 6 and nor should you!

Before we adopt the above conclusion we'd better confirm it by looking at the 2007 Canadian Lotto results shown in Chart 10.

Yes, you've probably guessed which one it is by now. Can you guess what we find? Why, of course, on no weeks were there three, four, five, or six numbers exactly divisible by 6 in the draw. This is getting to be serious proof. At last we are observing 100 percent certainty. I must say, it does inspire great confidence when we can positively avoid serious error in our future selections. After all, when we avoid error and mistakes in our selections, it automatically leaves us with the best possible chances. So, we can yet again tuck away another useful policy: *When choosing a line of future lottery numbers ensure that four, five, or six of them are not exactly divisible by 6.*

Help! This is Getting To Be Too Much!

You might be thinking that there is a lot of checking to do with each line you select. You're probably asking yourself, *will I remember what to do without having to read the book every time I want to make a selection?* Don't worry, there's a summary at the end of this book you can use, which will cut down on the thumbing through all the pages.

Better still, there is a computer program you can obtain (see the order form at the end of the book), and after entering your selections just one click checks your proposed entry in less than a second. You can even let the computer choose a line for you and this, too, is checked for validity!

CHART 11

UK 2007 SATURDAY RESULTS
ANALYSIS OF LOTTERY NUMBERS DIVISIBLE BY 7

WEEK No.	LOTTERY NUMBERS DRAWN						TOTAL IN WEEK	NUMBER OF TIMES PER WEEK IN YEAR						
								0	1	2	3	4	5	6
1	15	25	29	35	39	40	1	X	X	X	X			
2	05	08	12	20	28	48	1	X	X	X				
3	04	07	26	28	39	49	3	X	X	X				
4	04	15	21	23	24	38	1	X	X	X				
5	13	17	39	46	47	49	1	X	X	X				
6	22	26	38	39	41	42	1	X	X	X				
7	06	18	40	43	47	49	1	X	X	X				
8	05	18	26	34	42	49	2	X	X	X				
9	01	05	11	19	28	36	1	X	X	X				
10	01	09	16	34	38	41	0	X	X					
11	01	09	14	20	43	44	1	X	X					
12	09	14	26	28	30	45	2	X	X					
13	03	35	39	42	44	48	2	X	X					
14	23	24	30	31	33	37	0	X	X					
15	13	16	23	29	36	49	1	X	X					
16	14	20	21	30	41	46	2	X	X					
17	11	17	24	28	41	47	1	X	X					
18	04	33	34	38	39	49	1		X					
19	03	06	09	12	40	43	0		X					
20	17	19	20	32	36	48	0		X					
21	03	15	19	24	28	34	1		X					
22	01	10	33	35	38	43	1		X					
23	02	03	23	33	40	46	0		X					
24	08	17	33	41	43	45	0		X					
25	06	12	19	25	31	41	0		X					
26	10	11	17	34	38	46	0	17	25	9	1	0	0	0
27	16	22	28	30	33	35	2							
28	15	27	35	37	38	39	1							
29	03	10	21	25	29	49	2							
30	04	18	22	27	44	48	0							
31	12	23	25	26	34	49	1							
32	06	10	11	19	22	46	0							
33	02	12	26	32	37	47	0							
34	07	13	17	33	40	42	2							
35	03	27	34	41	42	48	1							
36	04	10	20	24	39	49	1							
37	03	07	12	21	25	36	2							
38	03	12	15	18	30	31	0							
39	01	09	10	11	16	49	1							
40	05	06	18	22	24	38	0							
41	07	11	12	36	38	39	1							
42	04	15	25	27	33	40	0							
43	06	08	10	13	22	32	0							
44	03	10	22	25	31	49	1							
45	05	11	13	18	25	35	1							
46	11	16	20	22	27	46	0							
47	01	14	25	37	39	47	1							
48	12	24	33	36	39	42	1							
49	04	06	10	11	24	33	0							
50	12	22	25	43	46	49	1							
51	11	13	14	16	21	44	2							
52	04	13	23	28	30	32	1							

Chapter 6
Considering Numbers Divisible by 7

LOOKING at Chart 11, you will notice first off, that in seventeen weeks of that year there were no numbers divisible by 7 drawn at all. That's about one third of a year; so, if you find in any of your selections that you have no numbers divisible by 7, there may be no need to worry. However, there were twenty-five weeks in that year where one of the numbers drawn was exactly divisible by 7. Also, there were nine weeks in that year where two of the numbers drawn were exactly divisible by 7. There was also one week of that year where three of the numbers drawn were exactly divisible by 7. Should you feel lucky, you could risk not having three numbers in your selections being divisible by 7 as there was only one instance of this in the year.

Added together, there were at least thirty-five weeks in 2007 where there was at least one number present that could be divided by 7. As that is most of the year, I would only tentatively advise including one number divisible by 7, as statistically it is not 100-percent certain. But the main point to note is that there were no weeks at all where four, five, or six of the numbers drawn were exactly divisible by 7. So, we can now recommend with complete confidence another important policy: *When choosing a line of future lottery numbers, ensure that four, five, or six of them are not exactly divisible by 7.*

Of course, we must verify that this policy is sound by checking with the Canadian Lotto results divided by 7, hence Chart 12.

CHART 12

CANADIAN LOTTO RESULTS 2007
ANALYSIS OF LOTTERY NUMBERS DIVIDED BY 7

WEEK No.	LOTTERY NUMBERS DRAWN						TOTAL IN WEEK	NUMBER OF TIMES PER WEEK IN YEAR						
								0	1	2	3	4	5	6
1	19	20	33	43	45	47	0	X	X	X	X			
2	01	02	03	19	25	41	0	X	X	X	X			
3	24	40	45	47	48	49	1	X	X	X				
4	06	09	17	20	22	40	0	X	X	X				
5	10	13	24	27	37	39	0	X	X	X				
6	08	13	23	37	41	42	1	X	X					
7	13	20	31	36	43	46	0	X	X					
8	04	06	15	33	38	40	0	X	X					
9	03	21	27	37	43	44	0	X	X					
10	09	18	28	37	42	49	3	X	X					
11	13	21	23	27	28	34	2	X	X					
12	01	13	19	26	32	46	0	X	X					
13	04	09	16	32	37	41	0	X	X					
14	10	12	23	26	35	37	1	X	X					
15	06	15	22	26	41	49	1	X	X					
16	17	29	33	43	45	49	1	X	X					
17	03	19	20	23	35	38	1	X	X					
18	01	23	26	28	33	40	1	X	X					
19	05	07	13	27	45	47	1	X	X					
20	08	16	33	37	40	42	1	X						
21	06	17	29	32	36	47	0	X						
22	08	16	19	32	40	46	0	X						
23	10	20	25	41	44	46	0	X						
24	03	15	31	33	43	48	0	X						
25	07	20	24	37	43	49	2	X						
26	06	12	25	43	45	47	0	X						
27	10	19	25	31	37	40	0	27	18	5	2	0	0	0
28	10	27	33	38	40	49	1							
29	09	10	22	29	38	41	0							
30	01	05	17	32	39	45	0							
31	09	17	18	20	41	49	1							
32	01	17	23	34	37	49	1							
33	02	12	32	34	38	48	0							
34	09	19	31	35	39	42	2							
35	11	17	18	28	31	46	1							
36	03	08	16	20	24	25	0							
37	09	39	40	43	46	48	0							
38	05	08	12	15	39	47	0							
39	09	19	26	29	39	45	0							
40	05	15	30	35	41	48	1							
41	01	26	30	32	39	47	0							
42	07	08	13	26	32	35	2							
43	12	13	17	34	40	47	0							
44	08	23	33	40	46	49	1							
45	03	13	14	17	20	42	2							
46	14	17	27	41	47	48	1							
47	01	10	25	27	30	36	0							
48	16	21	31	40	43	45	1							
49	02	09	11	22	35	45	1							
50	03	11	32	34	44	48	0							
51	08	17	30	36	40	47	0							
52	07	13	16	24	35	42	3							

22

In reviewing Chart 12, you will observe that there are hardly any numbers divided by 7 drawn in the year. Remember, it is not my intention to recommend what type of numbers to play. My recommendations consist of cautioning you on entering too many numbers of a certain type. Whether or not you should play some numbers divided by 7 is hard to say. What I can say with confidence after examining both charts is *When choosing a line of future lottery numbers, ensure that four, five, or six of them are not exactly divisible by 7.*

CHART 13

UK 2007 SATURDAY RESULTS
ANALYSIS OF LOTTERY NUMBERS DIVISIBLE BY 8

WEEK No.	LOTTERY NUMBERS DRAWN						TOTAL IN WEEK	NUMBER OF TIMES PER WEEK IN YEAR						
								0	1	2	3	4	5	6
1	15	25	29	35	39	40	0	X	X	X				
2	05	08	12	20	28	48	2	X	X	X				
3	04	07	26	28	39	49	0	X	X	X				
4	04	15	21	23	24	38	1	X	X					
5	13	17	39	46	47	49	0	X	X					
6	22	26	38	39	41	42	0	X	X					
7	06	18	40	43	47	49	1	X	X					
8	05	18	26	34	42	49	0	X	X					
9	01	05	11	19	28	36	0	X	X					
10	01	09	16	34	38	41	1	X	X					
11	01	09	14	20	43	44	0	X	X					
12	09	14	26	28	30	45	0	X	X					
13	03	35	39	42	44	48	0	X	X					
14	23	24	30	31	33	37	1	X	X					
15	13	16	23	29	36	49	1	X	X					
16	14	20	21	30	41	46	0	X	X					
17	11	17	24	28	41	47	1	X	X					
18	04	33	34	38	39	49	0	X	X					
19	03	06	09	12	40	43	1	X	X					
20	17	19	20	32	36	48	2	X	X					
21	03	15	19	24	28	34	1	X	X					
22	01	10	33	35	38	43	0	X	X					
23	02	03	23	33	40	46	1	X	X					
24	08	17	33	41	43	45	1	X	X					
25	06	12	19	25	31	41	0	X						
26	10	11	17	34	38	46	0	25	24	3	0	0	0	0
27	16	22	28	30	33	35	1							
28	15	27	35	37	38	39	0							
29	03	10	21	25	29	49	0							
30	04	18	22	27	44	48	1							
31	12	23	25	26	34	49	0							
32	06	10	11	19	22	46	0							
33	02	12	26	32	37	47	1							
34	07	13	17	33	40	42	1							
35	03	27	34	41	42	48	1							
36	04	10	20	24	39	49	1							
37	03	07	12	21	25	36	0							
38	03	12	15	18	30	31	0							
39	01	09	10	11	16	49	1							
40	05	06	18	22	24	38	1							
41	07	11	12	36	38	39	0							
42	04	15	25	27	33	40	1							
43	06	08	10	13	22	32	2							
44	03	10	22	25	31	49	0							
45	05	11	13	18	25	35	0							
46	11	16	20	22	27	46	1							
47	01	14	25	37	39	47	0							
48	12	24	33	36	39	42	1							
49	04	06	10	11	24	33	1							
50	12	22	25	43	46	49	0							
51	11	13	14	16	21	44	1							
52	04	13	23	28	30	32	1							

Chapter 7

Considering Numbers
Divisible by 8

THE same premise from the previous chapter holds true when we look at Chart 13 and evaluate it the same way, but for numbers divisible by 8. Employing the same strategies as we did above, we can safely come to the conclusion that it's a good idea *when choosing a line of future lottery numbers to ensure that three, four, five, or six of them are not divisible by 8,* but we now have to check Chart 14 *(next page)* of the Canadian Lotto results to make sure that this policy is sound.

I have to say at this point that the statistics seem to be pointing to the fact that it does *not* matter whether one uses numbers divisible by 8 in future selections. In 2007, there were twenty-five weeks of the U.K. Lottery where no numbers divisible by 8 were drawn. In the same year of the Canadian Lotto, there were twenty-two weeks where no numbers divisible by 8 were drawn. Therefore, the only solid piece of advice one could draw from both charts is that *When choosing a line of future lottery numbers, ensure that four, five, or six of them are not divisible by 8.*

CHART 14

CANADIAN LOTTO RESULTS 2007
ANALYSIS OF LOTTERY NUMBERS DIVISIBLE BY 8

WEEK No.	LOTTERY NUMBERS DRAWN						TOTAL IN WEEK	NUMBER OF TIMES PER WEEK IN YEAR						
								0	1	2	3	4	5	6
1	19	20	33	43	45	47	0	X	X	X	X	X		
2	01	02	03	19	25	41	0	X	X	X	X			
3	24	40	45	47	48	49	3	X	X	X	X			
4	06	09	17	20	22	40	1	X	X	X				
5	10	13	24	27	37	39	1	X	X	X				
6	08	13	23	37	41	42	1	X	X	X				
7	13	20	31	36	43	46	0	X	X	X				
8	04	06	15	33	38	40	1	X	X	X				
9	03	21	27	37	43	44	0	X	X	X				
10	09	18	28	37	42	49	0	X	X					
11	13	21	23	27	28	34	0	X	X					
12	01	13	19	26	32	46	1	X	X					
13	04	09	16	32	37	41	2	X	X					
14	10	12	23	26	35	37	0	X	X					
15	06	15	22	26	41	49	0	X	X					
16	17	29	33	43	45	49	0	X	X					
17	03	19	20	23	35	38	0	X	X					
18	01	23	26	28	33	40	1	X						
19	05	07	13	27	45	47	0	X						
20	08	16	33	37	40	42	3	X						
21	06	17	29	32	36	47	1	X						
22	08	16	19	32	40	46	4	X						
23	10	20	25	41	44	46	0	22	17	9	3	1	0	0
24	03	15	31	33	43	48	1							
25	07	20	24	37	43	49	1							
26	06	12	25	43	45	47	0							
27	10	19	25	31	37	40	1							
28	10	27	33	38	40	49	1							
29	09	10	22	29	38	41	0							
30	01	05	17	32	39	45	1							
31	09	17	18	20	41	49	0							
32	01	17	23	34	37	49	0							
33	02	12	32	34	38	48	2							
34	09	19	31	35	39	42	0							
35	11	17	18	28	31	46	0							
36	03	08	16	20	24	25	3							
37	09	39	40	43	46	48	2							
38	05	08	12	15	39	47	1							
39	09	19	26	29	39	45	0							
40	05	15	30	35	41	48	1							
41	01	26	30	32	39	47	1							
42	07	08	13	26	32	35	2							
43	12	13	17	34	40	47	1							
44	08	23	33	40	46	49	2							
45	03	13	14	17	20	42	0							
46	14	17	27	41	47	48	1							
47	01	10	25	27	30	36	0							
48	16	21	31	40	43	45	2							
49	02	09	11	22	35	45	0							
50	03	11	32	34	44	48	2							
51	08	17	30	36	40	47	2							
52	07	13	16	24	35	42	2							

Chapter 8

Considering Numbers
Divisible by 9

MOVING on to Chart 15 *(next page)*, we are again looking at the 2007 U.K. Lottery results. As before, we can not say one way or the other whether to pick any numbers divisible by 9. Most weeks in the year, thirty-one in fact, never featured one of these numbers at all. There are only five numbers available that are evenly divisible by 9 (9, 18, 27, 36, and 45), hence the low frequency of these numbers being drawn. You will notice in the diagram that there is no zero statement under the 6 column, there is merely a dash indicating a non-applicable status.

We can, however, come to some sort of policy indicated by Chart 15. We can say that *when choosing a line of future lottery numbers, ensure that three, four, or five of them are not divisible by 9.* But, as usual, in order to be sure we are correct in our policy we need to examine the results of the Canadian Lotto. So, on to Chart 16 *(next page)*.

Applying our strategies as we did in all previous charts, we can confirm the observations of Chart 15 and say with certainty that: *When choosing a line of future lottery numbers ensure that three, four, or five of them are not divisible by 9.*

27

CHART 15

UK 2007 SATURDAY RESULTS
ANALYSIS OF LOTTERY NUMBERS DIVISIBLE BY 9

WEEK No.	LOTTERY NUMBERS DRAWN						TOTAL IN WEEK	NUMBER OF TIMES PER WEEK IN YEAR						
								0	1	2	3	4	5	6
1	15	25	29	35	39	40	0	X	X	X				
2	05	08	12	20	28	48	0	X	X	X				
3	04	07	26	28	39	49	0	X	X					
4	04	15	21	23	24	38	0	X	X					
5	13	17	39	46	47	49	0	X	X					
6	22	26	38	39	41	42	0	X	X					
7	06	18	40	43	47	49	1	X	X					
8	05	18	26	34	42	49	1	X	X					
9	01	05	11	19	28	36	1	X	X					
10	01	09	16	34	38	41	1	X	X					
11	01	09	14	20	43	44	1	X	X					
12	09	14	26	28	30	45	2	X	X					
13	03	35	39	42	44	48	0	X	X					
14	23	24	30	31	33	37	0	X	X					
15	13	16	23	29	36	49	1	X	X					
16	14	20	21	30	41	46	0	X	X					
17	11	17	24	28	41	47	0	X	X					
18	04	33	34	38	39	49	0	X	X					
19	03	06	09	12	40	43	1	X	X					
20	17	19	20	32	36	48	1	X						
21	03	15	19	24	28	34	0	X						
22	01	10	33	35	38	43	0	X						
23	02	03	23	33	40	46	0	X						
24	08	17	33	41	43	45	1	X						
25	06	12	19	25	31	41	0	X						
26	10	11	17	34	38	46	0	X						
27	16	22	28	30	33	35	0	X						
28	15	27	35	37	38	39	1	X						
29	03	10	21	25	29	49	0	X						
30	04	18	22	27	44	48	2	X						
31	12	23	25	26	34	49	0	X						
32	06	10	11	19	22	46	0	30	20	2	0	0	0	-
33	02	12	26	32	37	47	0							
34	07	13	17	33	40	42	0							
35	03	27	34	41	42	48	1							
36	04	10	20	24	39	49	0							
37	03	07	12	21	25	36	1							
38	03	12	15	18	30	31	1							
39	01	09	10	11	16	49	1							
40	05	06	18	22	24	38	1							
41	07	11	12	36	38	39	1							
42	04	15	25	27	33	40	1							
43	06	08	10	13	22	32	0							
44	03	10	22	25	31	49	0							
45	05	11	13	18	25	35	1							
46	11	16	20	22	27	46	1							
47	01	14	25	37	39	47	0							
48	12	24	33	36	39	42	1							
49	04	06	10	11	24	33	0							
50	12	22	25	43	46	49	0							
51	11	13	14	16	21	44	0							
52	04	13	23	28	30	32	0							

CHART 16

CANADIAN LOTTO RESULTS 2007
ANALYSIS OF LOTTERY NUMBERS DIVISIBLE BY 9

WEEK No.	LOTTERY NUMBERS DRAWN						TOTAL IN WEEK	0	1	2	3	4	5	6
1	19	20	33	43	45	47	1	X	X	X				
2	01	02	03	19	25	41	0	X	X	X				
3	24	40	45	47	48	49	1	X	X	X				
4	06	09	17	20	22	40	1	X	X	X				
5	10	13	24	27	37	39	1	X	X	X				
6	08	13	23	37	41	42	0	X	X					
7	13	20	31	36	43	46	1	X	X					
8	04	06	15	33	38	40	0	X	X					
9	03	21	27	37	43	44	1	X	X					
10	09	18	28	37	42	49	2	X	X					
11	13	21	23	27	28	34	1	X	X					
12	01	13	19	26	32	46	0	X	X					
13	04	09	16	32	37	41	1	X	X					
14	10	12	23	26	35	37	0	X	X					
15	06	15	22	26	41	49	0	X	X					
16	17	29	33	43	45	49	1	X	X					
17	03	19	20	23	35	38	0	X	X					
18	01	23	26	28	33	40	0	X	X					
19	05	07	13	27	45	47	1	X	X					
20	08	16	33	37	40	42	0	X	X					
21	06	17	29	32	36	47	1	X	X					
22	08	16	19	32	40	46	0	X						
23	10	20	25	41	44	46	0	X						
24	03	15	31	33	43	48	0	X						
25	07	20	24	37	43	49	0	X						
26	06	12	25	43	45	47	1	X						
27	10	19	25	31	37	40	0	26	21	5	0	0	0	-
28	10	27	33	38	40	49	1							
29	09	10	22	29	38	41	1							
30	01	05	17	32	39	45	1							
31	09	17	18	20	41	49	2							
32	01	17	23	34	37	49	0							
33	02	12	32	34	38	48	0							
34	09	19	31	35	39	42	1							
35	11	17	18	28	31	46	1							
36	03	08	16	20	24	25	0							
37	09	39	40	43	46	48	1							
38	05	08	12	15	39	47	0							
39	09	19	26	29	39	45	2							
40	05	15	30	35	41	48	0							
41	01	26	30	32	39	47	0							
42	07	08	13	26	32	35	0							
43	12	13	17	34	40	47	0							
44	08	23	33	40	46	49	0							
45	03	13	14	17	20	42	0							
46	14	17	27	41	47	48	1							
47	01	10	25	27	30	36	2							
48	16	21	31	40	43	45	1							
49	02	09	11	22	35	45	2							
50	03	11	32	34	44	48	0							
51	08	17	30	36	40	47	1							
52	07	13	16	24	35	42	0							

CHART 17

UK 2007 SATURDAY RESULTS
ANALYSIS OF LOTTERY NUMBERS DIVISIBLE BY 10

WEEK No.	LOTTERY NUMBERS DRAWN						TOTAL IN WEEK	NUMBER OF TIMES PER WEEK IN YEAR						
								0	1	2	3	4	5	6
1	15	25	29	35	39	40	1	X	X	X				
2	05	08	12	20	28	48	1	X	X	X				
3	04	07	26	28	39	49	0	X	X					
4	04	15	21	23	24	38	0	X	X					
5	13	17	39	46	47	49	0	X	X					
6	22	26	38	39	41	42	0	X	X					
7	06	18	40	43	47	49	1	X	X					
8	05	18	26	34	42	49	0	X	X					
9	01	05	11	19	28	36	0	X	X					
10	01	09	16	34	38	41	0	X	X					
11	01	09	14	20	43	44	1	X	X					
12	09	14	26	28	30	45	1	X	X					
13	03	35	39	42	44	48	0	X	X					
14	23	24	30	31	33	37	1	X	X					
15	13	16	23	29	36	49	0	X	X					
16	14	20	21	30	41	46	2	X	X					
17	11	17	24	28	41	47	0	X	X					
18	04	33	34	38	39	49	0	X	X					
19	03	06	09	12	40	43	1	X	X					
20	17	19	20	32	36	48	1	X	X					
21	03	15	19	24	28	34	0	X	X					
22	01	10	33	35	38	43	1	X	X					
23	02	03	23	33	40	46	1	X	X					
24	08	17	33	41	43	45	0	X						
25	06	12	19	25	31	41	0	X						
26	10	11	17	34	38	46	1	X						
27	16	22	28	30	33	35	1	X						
28	15	27	35	37	38	39	0	27	23	2	0	0	-	-
29	03	10	21	25	29	49	1							
30	04	18	22	27	44	48	0							
31	12	23	25	26	34	49	0							
32	06	10	11	19	22	46	1							
33	02	12	26	32	37	47	0							
34	07	13	17	33	40	42	1							
35	03	27	34	41	42	48	0							
36	04	10	20	24	39	49	2							
37	03	07	12	21	25	36	0							
38	03	12	15	18	30	31	1							
39	01	09	10	11	16	49	1							
40	05	06	18	22	24	38	0							
41	07	11	12	36	38	39	0							
42	04	15	25	27	33	40	1							
43	06	08	10	13	22	32	1							
44	03	10	22	25	31	49	1							
45	05	11	13	18	25	35	0							
46	11	16	20	22	27	46	1							
47	01	14	25	37	39	47	0							
48	12	24	33	36	39	42	0							
49	04	06	10	11	24	33	1							
50	12	22	25	43	46	49	0							
51	11	13	14	16	21	44	0							
52	04	13	23	28	30	32	1							

Chapter 9

Considering Numbers Divisible by 10, 11, and 12

I suspect that division by 10 will have the same future policy as that of division by 11 or 12. This is because there are four numbers in any six-out-of forty-nine lottery that are divisible by 10 (10, 20, 30, and 40), four numbers divisible by 11 (11, 22, 33, and 44), and four numbers divisible by 12 (12, 24, 36, and 48).

We will examine only the charts that show division by 10 and apply the results of the examination to the policies of 11 and 12. To do that, let's look at Chart 17. These are the results of the 2007 U.K. National Lottery, with numbers divisible by 10 highlighted. You will recall that we intend to apply the lessons learned to numbers divisible by 11 and 12 also. Statistically that is an okay thing to do.

Straight away we can tell by looking at the chart that we should never include in our future lottery selections a line that includes more than two numbers divisible by 10. You know the form by now! We have to check the validity of this by examining the Canadian Lotto results with the numbers divisible by 10 highlighted. Hence, Chart 18 *(next page)*.

From this chart, we see that the number 10 occurred nine times, 20 occurred six times, 30 occurred six times, and 40 occurred six times. Some of you might conclude that 10 is a hot number showing up 9 times that year. Be cautioned, some lottery consultants say that one should always choose a hot number (a number that has been drawn many times), but

CHART 18

CANADIAN LOTTO RESULTS 2007
ANALYSIS OF LOTTERY NUMBERS DIVISIBLE BY 10

WEEK No.	LOTTERY NUMBERS DRAWN						TOTAL IN WEEK	NUMBER OF TIMES PER WEEK IN YEAR						
								0	1	2	3	4	5	6
1	19	20	33	43	45	47	1	X	X	X				
2	01	02	03	19	25	41	0	X	X	X				
3	24	40	45	47	48	49	1	X	X	X				
4	06	09	17	20	22	40	2	X	X	X				
5	10	13	24	27	37	39	1	X	X	X				
6	08	13	23	37	41	42	0	X	X	X				
7	13	20	31	36	43	46	1	X	X					
8	04	06	15	33	38	40	1	X	X					
9	03	21	27	37	43	44	0	X	X					
10	09	18	28	37	42	49	0	X	X					
11	13	21	23	27	28	34	0	X	X					
12	01	13	19	26	32	46	0	X	X					
13	04	09	16	32	37	41	0	X	X					
14	10	12	23	26	35	37	1	X	X					
15	06	15	22	26	41	49	0	X	X					
16	17	29	33	43	45	49	0	X	X					
17	03	19	20	23	35	38	1	X	X					
18	01	23	26	28	33	40	1	X	X					
19	05	07	13	27	45	47	0	X	X					
20	08	16	33	37	40	42	1	X	X					
21	06	17	29	32	36	47	0	X	X					
22	08	16	19	32	40	46	1	X						
23	10	20	25	41	44	46	2	X						
24	03	15	31	33	43	48	0	X						
25	07	20	24	37	43	49	1	X						
26	06	12	25	43	45	47	0	25	21	6	0	0	-	-
27	10	19	25	31	37	40	2							
28	10	27	33	38	40	49	2							
29	09	10	22	29	38	41	1							
30	01	05	17	32	39	45	0							
31	09	17	18	20	41	49	1							
32	01	17	23	34	37	49	0							
33	02	12	32	34	38	48	0							
34	09	19	31	35	39	42	0							
35	11	17	18	28	31	46	0							
36	03	08	16	20	24	25	1							
37	09	39	40	43	46	48	1							
38	05	08	12	15	39	47	0							
39	09	19	26	29	39	45	0							
40	05	15	30	35	41	48	1							
41	01	26	30	32	39	47	1							
42	07	08	13	26	32	35	0							
43	12	13	17	34	40	47	1							
44	08	23	33	40	46	49	1							
45	03	13	14	17	20	42	1							
46	14	17	27	41	47	48	0							
47	01	10	25	27	30	36	2							
48	16	21	31	40	43	45	1							
49	02	09	11	22	35	45	0							
50	03	11	32	34	44	48	0							
51	08	17	30	36	40	47	2							
52	07	13	16	24	35	42	0							

others say that one should *not* choose a hot number in order to maintain the laws of averages. This is clearly a contradiction and so should be ignored. The same goes for cold numbers (those that have not been picked in a long time). In any case, the balls simply do not have any memory of previous results and therefore have absolutely no influence on future drawings.

Chart 18 is quite similar to Chart 17 in that it shows no selections divisible by 10 chosen about half the time. This means that no recommendation can be made as to whether or not to numbers divisible by 10 in your selections. The charts do show, however, that you should not select three or four numbers divisible by 10. (Note that there are not five or six numbers available to select in the draw, as the numbers in our analysis only go up to 49.)

You will recall that there are four numbers divisible by ten and four numbers divisible by eleven and twelve each. This means we can statistically apply the policy for division by 10 to that of division by 11 and division by 12, also. This makes it safe to say that *when choosing a line of future lottery numbers, ensure that three or four of them are not divisible by 10, 11, or 12.*

CHART 19

UK 2007 SATURDAY RESULTS
ANALYSIS OF LOTTERY NUMBERS DIVISIBLE BY 13

WEEK No.	LOTTERY NUMBERS DRAWN						TOTAL IN WEEK	NUMBER OF TIMES PER WEEK IN YEAR						
								0	1	2	3	4	5	6
1	15	25	29	35	39	40	1	X	X	X				
2	05	08	12	20	28	48	0	X	X	X				
3	04	07	26	28	39	49	2	X	X	X				
4	04	15	21	23	24	38	0	X	X					
5	13	17	39	46	47	49	2	X	X					
6	22	26	38	39	41	42	2	X	X					
7	06	18	40	43	47	49	0	X	X					
8	05	18	26	34	42	49	1	X	X					
9	01	05	11	19	28	36	0	X	X					
10	01	09	16	34	38	41	0	X	X					
11	01	09	14	20	43	44	0	X	X					
12	09	14	26	28	30	45	1	X	X					
13	03	35	39	42	44	48	1	X	X					
14	23	24	30	31	33	37	0	X	X					
15	13	16	23	29	36	49	1	X	X					
16	14	20	21	30	41	46	0	X	X					
17	11	17	24	28	41	47	0	X	X					
18	04	33	34	38	39	49	1	X	X					
19	03	06	09	12	40	43	0	X						
20	17	19	20	32	36	48	0	X						
21	03	15	19	24	28	34	0	X						
22	01	10	33	35	38	43	0	X						
23	02	03	23	33	40	46	0	X						
24	08	17	33	41	43	45	0	X						
25	06	12	19	25	31	41	0	X						
26	10	11	17	34	38	46	0	X						
27	16	22	28	30	33	35	0	X						
28	15	27	35	37	38	39	1	X						
29	03	10	21	25	29	49	0	X						
30	04	18	22	27	44	48	0	X						
31	12	23	25	26	34	49	1	X						
32	06	10	11	19	22	46	0	34	15	3	0	-	-	-
33	02	12	26	32	37	47	1							
34	07	13	17	33	40	42	1							
35	03	27	34	41	42	48	0							
36	04	10	20	24	39	49	1							
37	03	07	12	21	25	36	0							
38	03	12	15	18	30	31	0							
39	01	09	10	11	16	49	0							
40	05	06	18	22	24	38	0							
41	07	11	12	36	38	39	1							
42	04	15	25	27	33	40	0							
43	06	08	10	13	22	32	1							
44	03	10	22	25	31	49	0							
45	05	11	13	18	25	35	1							
46	11	16	20	22	27	46	0							
47	01	14	25	37	39	47	1							
48	12	24	33	36	39	42	1							
49	04	06	10	11	24	33	0							
50	12	22	25	43	46	49	0							
51	11	13	14	16	21	44	1							
52	04	13	23	28	30	32	1							

Chapter 10
Considering Numbers Divisible by 13 (and 14, 15, and 16)

HAVE a look at Chart 19. This diagram relates to the 2007 U.K. National Lottery where the numbers are analysed for division by 13. There are three numbers present in the six-out-of-forty-nine lotteries that are divisible by 13: 13, 26, and 39. There are also three numbers present in these lotteries that are divisible by 14 (14, 28, and 42), 15 (15, 30, and 45), and 16 (16, 32, and 48).

After analyzing Chart 19, we will apply the policy formulated to division by the numbers 14, 15, and 16. It is statistically sound to do this, as there are three numbers present of each of the types mentioned.

No doubt you can sense that we are reaching the margins of uncertainty for our future actions. This applies especially to whether or not to employ these numbers in our selections. Nevertheless, we can at least be reasonably confident that *When choosing a line of future lottery numbers, we should ensure that three of them are not exactly divisible by 13.*

But, first we will confirm this finding by analysing the 2007 Canadian Lotto results in Chart 20 *(next page)*. It is quite obvious that our approach to formulating viable policies is quite correct. Chart 20 is very similar to Chart 19 and so we can go ahead and conclude that *when choosing a line of future lottery numbers, it is best to ensure that three of them are not exactly divisible by 13, 14, 15, or 16.*

CHART 20

CANADIAN LOTTO RESULTS 2007
ANALYSIS OF LOTTERY NUMBERS DIVISIBLE BY 13

WEEK No.	LOTTERY NUMBERS DRAWN						TOTAL IN WEEK	NUMBER OF TIMES PER WEEK IN YEAR						
								0	1	2	3	4	5	6
1	19	20	33	43	45	47	0	X	X	X				
2	01	02	03	19	25	41	0	X	X	X				
3	24	40	45	47	48	49	0	X	X	X				
4	06	09	17	20	22	40	0	X	X	X				
5	10	13	24	27	37	39	2	X	X	X				
6	08	13	23	37	41	42	1	X	X					
7	13	20	31	36	43	46	1	X	X					
8	04	06	15	33	38	40	0	X	X					
9	03	21	27	37	43	44	0	X	X					
10	09	18	28	37	42	49	0	X	X					
11	13	21	23	27	28	34	1	X	X					
12	01	13	19	26	32	46	2	X	X					
13	04	09	16	32	37	41	0	X	X					
14	10	12	23	26	35	37	1	X						
15	06	15	22	26	41	49	1	X						
16	17	29	33	43	45	49	0	X						
17	03	19	20	23	35	38	0	X						
18	01	23	26	28	33	40	1	X						
19	05	07	13	27	45	47	1	X						
20	08	16	33	37	40	42	0	X						
21	06	17	29	32	36	47	0	X						
22	08	16	19	32	40	46	0	X						
23	10	20	25	41	44	46	0	X						
24	03	15	31	33	43	48	0	X						
25	07	20	24	37	43	49	0	X						
26	06	12	25	43	45	47	0	X						
27	10	19	25	31	37	40	0	X						
28	10	27	33	38	40	49	0	X						
29	09	10	22	29	38	41	0	X						
30	01	05	17	32	39	45	1	X						
31	09	17	18	20	41	49	0	X						
32	01	17	23	34	37	49	0	X						
33	02	12	32	34	38	48	0	X						
34	09	19	31	35	39	42	1	X						
35	11	17	18	28	31	46	0	34	13	5	0	-	-	-
36	03	08	16	20	24	25	0							
37	09	39	40	43	46	48	0							
38	05	08	12	15	39	47	1							
39	09	19	26	29	39	45	2							
40	05	15	30	35	41	48	0							
41	01	26	30	32	39	47	2							
42	07	08	13	26	32	35	2							
43	12	13	17	34	40	47	1							
44	08	23	33	40	46	49	0							
45	03	13	14	17	20	42	1							
46	14	17	27	41	47	48	0							
47	01	10	25	27	30	36	0							
48	16	21	31	40	43	45	0							
49	02	09	11	22	35	45	0							
50	03	11	32	34	44	48	0							
51	08	17	30	36	40	47	0							
52	07	13	16	24	35	42	1							

Chapter 11

Considering Numbers
Divisible by 17 through 24

THE next set of numbers to consider are those that divisible by 17, 18, 19, 20, 21, 22, 23, and 24. Each of these numbers has only one multiple (e.g. 17 and 34, 18 and 36, etc.), therefore, there are only two numbers in the six-out-of-forty-nine lottery that are divisible by 17. The same holds true for the numbers 18 through 24. I examined the charts and noticed that sometimes both multiples of these numbers were present in any one week of the draw. Because of this, it can be presumed that there is no value whatsoever in trying to formulate a policy covering the multiples of 17 to 24. This negative conclusion represents the limit to this particular line of investigation. However, there are many other important lines of investigation that we can examine and use to our advantage.

Chapter 12

Considering Numbers that Have Personal Connections

THE numbers selected by any lottery machine are truly chaotically cho-sen and are completely random. You can rely on that being a cast-iron fact. But people, being what they are, tend to fly in the face of facts. For example, you might imagine that there is some merit in choosing your numbers by birth dates, home addresses, or some order or pattern. This is what most people I know do.

Choosing lottery numbers based on birth dates introduces a near-fatal mathematical restriction to numbers covering those from 1 through 31. This might satisfy some people's emotional need, but it does virtually nothing to place them in line for a jackpot. Have they never understood that the numbers 31 through 49 are almost always drawn as part of most jackpot wins?!

If you view your entries as a bit of fun, then go ahead and have a good time. But, don't waste your time reading this book! This book is meant to help you win money, that's all. There is no other agenda.

Then there is the method of choosing house numbers. This auto-matically introduces a bias to the lower numbers. The street numbers, of course, usually start at 1, but they don't always finish up at 49. Streets very often finish their sequence of numbers before that. You can see that this means there are fewer houses in the range of 40 to 49 than there are in the range of 1 to 10.

Choosing numbers based on patterns is the craziest method of all, statistically speaking. I have examined literally hundreds of patterns and they never feature in jackpot draws. This whole book examines the most common patterns and actually proves to your satisfaction that using number patterns in your lottery choices is completely wrong.

So, how do you set about generating a set of random numbers for your lottery selection? One way would be to use an electronic device such as a computer or scientific calculator with a random number generator built in. This may be okay, but I have to say that the methods used by these devises in generating random numbers are not perfect. In the design of calculators and computer operating systems, a large list of about 65,000 numbers is used. So, they are not actually random. Mathematicians call the results from these devices quasi-random numbers.

The analysis in this book leads always to one objective: remove all vestiges of pattern and order from your selections. This is bound to leave you with complete and total chaotic random selections. They are your winning lottery selections.

An acceptable method of selecting your lottery numbers might be by using one those devices that look like rattles. They have forty-nine small, numbered balls in them. After a swift rattle, six settle out randomly. Although these types of devices are better than a deliberate choice, I have to caution you that you would still need to check the validity of those results by going through all the checks shown in this book.

Having already said that choosing house numbers or birth dates as a means of selecting your lottery numbers is not a good thing, I have to say that it is still possible to do this provided you confine your fixed choice to three or four numbers only. You can then add other numbers to the group so that the whole group then passes all the validity tests shown in this book.

For example, confining your selection to birthdays might give you a selection consisting of 3, 5, 17, 19, 24, and 27. (These are actually birthdays from my own family.) Notice that there are no numbers in the 30s or 40s series. This would invalidate all chances of a jackpot for any year you care to choose.

You will see later on that the sixth number (when placed in ascending order) of any lottery draw is almost always 30 or above. Yes, I realize that on one occasion the sixth number was as low as 25, but I consider this a freak result. (We will examine this aspect in yet another chart later on.)

So, mixing in a few random numbers among my family's birthday numbers might yield 3, 5, 14, 22, 30, and 44. This would have won the U.K. jackpot. A much better prospect!

Chapter 13

Considering Numbers Divisible by a Common Number

WE are now nearly halfway through this book and I bet you're groaning at the prospect of all the checking I am suggesting should be done. Remember to help you do all the necessary checking, I have a written a computer program that does it for you in a trice! Go to the www.lotteryhelp.com site to obtain this software. I remind you of this facility because I am about to unleash yet another vast new range of checking procedures on you.

Consider the selection 3, 9, 12, 24, 36, and 45. All these numbers are divisible by 3 and will never occur, as there is too much order in the selection *(see page 4)*. But what about 5, 11, 14, 26, 38, and 47? None are divisible by a common number, so they appear to be acceptable. But if you reduce each number by 2, this returns you to the values of the previous sequence, which are all divisible by 3. This means that the second sequence is just as invalid a selection as the first.

I Can Help You!

My computer program has all these special checks incorporated. Yes, to do all the validity checking outlined in this book by hand is an awesome task and you do really need my computer program to help you, especially if you intend to check a great many proposed lines. The order form for the validity-checking program is at the back of this book.

I have not proven this to you in another chart, but rest assured I have checked this concept thoroughly and these incremented sequences are not random and should also be avoided like the plague!

My computer program makes checking your selections easy, but if you don't have a computer to help you, don't despair! There is an abbreviated list of the most obvious checking procedures at the end of this book. Believe me, working through the list is vital if you are to stand any chance at all of winning. It may take some time, but I assure you it will be worth it. And, if you intend to keep your selections fixed, you only need to do the checking once!

CHART 21

UK 2007 SATURDAY RESULTS
ANALYSIS OF LOTTERY NUMBERS IN THE UNITS' SERIES

WEEK No.	LOTTERY NUMBERS DRAWN	TOTAL IN WEEK	0	1	2	3	4	5	6
			NUMBER OF TIMES PER WEEK IN YEAR						
1	15 25 29 35 39 40	0	X	X	X	X			
2	05 08 12 20 28 48	2	X	X	X				
3	04 07 26 28 39 49	2	X	X	X				
4	04 15 21 23 24 38	1	X	X	X				
5	13 17 39 46 47 49	0	X	X	X				
6	22 26 38 39 41 42	0	X	X	X				
7	06 18 40 43 47 49	1	X	X	X				
8	05 18 26 34 42 49	1	X	X	X				
9	01 05 11 19 28 36	2	X	X	X				
10	01 09 16 34 38 41	2	X	X	X				
11	01 09 14 20 43 44	2	X	X	X				
12	09 14 26 28 30 45	1	X	X					
13	03 35 39 42 44 48	1	X	X					
14	23 24 30 31 33 37	0	X	X					
15	13 16 23 29 36 49	0	X	X					
16	14 20 21 30 41 46	0	X	X					
17	11 17 24 28 41 47	0		X					
18	04 33 34 38 39 49	1		X					
19	03 06 09 12 40 43	3		X					
20	17 19 20 32 36 48	0		X					
21	03 15 19 24 28 34	1		X					
22	01 10 33 35 38 43	1		X					
23	02 03 23 33 40 46	2		X					
24	08 17 33 41 43 45	1		X					
25	06 12 19 25 31 41	1	16	24	11	1	0	0	0
26	10 11 17 34 38 46	0							
27	16 22 28 30 33 35	0							
28	15 27 35 37 38 39	0							
29	03 10 21 25 29 49	1							
30	04 18 22 27 44 48	1							
31	12 23 25 26 34 49	0							
32	06 10 11 19 22 46	1							
33	02 12 26 32 37 47	1							
34	07 13 17 33 40 42	1							
35	03 27 34 41 42 48	1							
36	04 10 20 24 39 49	1							
37	03 07 12 21 25 36	2							
38	03 12 15 18 30 31	1							
39	01 09 10 11 16 49	2							
40	05 06 18 22 24 38	2							
41	07 11 12 36 38 39	1							
42	04 15 25 27 33 40	1							
43	06 08 10 13 22 32	2							
44	03 10 22 25 31 49	1							
45	05 11 13 18 25 35	1							
46	11 16 20 22 27 46	0							
47	01 14 25 37 39 47	1							
48	12 24 33 36 39 42	0							
49	04 06 10 11 24 33	2							
50	12 22 25 43 46 49	0							
51	11 13 14 16 21 44	0							
52	04 13 23 28 30 32	1							

Chapter 14

Considering Numbers in the Units Series

HERE'S another check. Have a look at Chart 21, which analyzes the occurrences of the numbers ranging from 1 through 9 on the weekly draws from the 2007 National Lottery results. This is the familiar units series. It is not a specially ordered sequence ranging up from 1 to 49, but a tight incremental sequence rising by one. Analyzing groupings of numbers like these happens to yield beneficial results. It is easy to follow, see for yourself:-

- In sixteen weeks of 2007, there were no numbers from the units series present at all.
- In twenty-four weeks of that year, there was one number from the units series present.
- In eleven weeks of that year there were two numbers from the units series present.
- In only one week of that year there were three numbers from the units series present.
- There was never a week where there were four, five, or six numbers from the units series present.

Looking at the last observation makes me think of those who actually choose to select all their numbers from the units series. Believe it or not, the selection 1, 2, 3, 4, 5, and 6 is very popular. In fact, there are at least 20,000 people weekly in the United Kingdom who select that very sequence on the grounds that it shares the same odds of winning, 1 in about

14,000,000, as any other sequence. Serious professional mathematicians share this view also. I do despair for the human race sometimes!

Look at the above results again very closely and consider the following:
- Four units in a line hasn't happened (and won't).
- Five units in a line hasn't happened (and won't).
- Six units in a line hasn't happened (and won't).

Incidentally, in the highly unlikely event of the sequence 1 through 6 ever coming up, those 20,000 or more unfortunate, misguided punters would receive only £200 each, even if the jackpot was £4,000,000. That's not much of a reward for waiting at least 14,000,000 weeks! I presume we all are interested in achieving a big win within a shorter time frame than that? If so, read on.

As the above three observations are obvious cast-iron facts, we should be able to propose yet another viable policy based on this solid evidence—*when choosing a line of future lottery numbers, ensure that four, five, or six of them are not in the units series.* But, we should check with the Canadian 2007 Lotto results and Chart 22 to make sure first.

What does this chart say about we have done had we taken notice of the advice from the previous chart? Well, we would have been 100-percent correct! You see, not one of the 4, 5, or 6 column scored anything at all. This is exactly the same as the 2007 U.K. Lottery analysis. Never was there a week with four, five, or six numbers in the units' series chosen. We can therefore confirm, with absolute confidence, that the best advice to follow as far as the units' series is concerned is: ***When choosing a line of future lottery numbers, ensure that four, five, or six of them are not in the units series.***

I see a bit of space left on this page so I'll give some examples of what I mean…

If you choose 1, 2, 3, 4, 9, and 41 as your lottery selection the numbers, you probably would not win. Five of these are in the units series. You can almost feel that this set of numbers is wrong.

If you choose as your lottery selection 1, 3, 4, 9, 22, and 41, then you would probably still would not win. Four of these numbers are in the units series. If you replaced any of the units with any other type of number in the tens series or above, then this would be acceptable.

If you insist that your choice of your lottery numbers be 1, 2, 3, 4, 6, and 9 then, I say, "Good day to you." I can't help you if you won't listen. I am quite sure that, by now, you have assimilated the lessons shown to you and will employ the policies given. Basically it's a choice between wrong theory and practical reality. I would go for practical reality every time.

CHART 22

CANADIAN LOTTO RESULTS 2007
ANALYSIS OF LOTTERY NUMBERS IN THE UNITS' SERIES

WEEK No.	LOTTERY NUMBERS DRAWN						TOTAL IN WEEK	NUMBER OF TIMES PER WEEK IN YEAR						
								0	1	2	3	4	5	6
1	19	20	33	43	45	47	0	X	X	X	X			
2	01	02	03	19	25	41	3	X	X	X				
3	24	40	45	47	48	49	0	X	X	X				
4	06	09	17	20	22	40	2	X	X	X				
5	10	13	24	27	37	39	0	X	X	X				
6	08	13	23	37	41	42	1	X	X	X				
7	13	20	31	36	43	46	0	X	X	X				
8	04	06	15	33	38	40	2	X	X	X				
9	03	21	27	37	43	44	1	X	X	X				
10	09	18	28	37	42	49	1	X	X					
11	13	21	23	27	28	34	0	X	X					
12	01	13	19	26	32	46	1	X	X					
13	04	09	16	32	37	41	2	X	X					
14	10	12	23	26	35	37	0	X	X					
15	06	15	22	26	41	49	1		X					
16	17	29	33	43	45	49	0		X					
17	03	19	20	23	35	38	1		X					
18	01	23	26	28	33	40	1		X					
19	05	07	13	27	45	47	2		X					
20	08	16	33	37	40	42	1		X					
21	06	17	29	32	36	47	1		X					
22	08	16	19	32	40	46	1		X					
23	10	20	25	41	44	46	0		X					
24	03	15	31	33	43	48	1		X					
25	07	20	24	37	43	49	1		X					
26	06	12	25	43	45	47	1		X					
27	10	19	25	31	37	40	0		X					
28	10	27	33	38	40	49	0		X					
29	09	10	22	29	38	41	1	14	28	9	1	0	0	0
30	01	05	17	32	39	45	2							
31	09	17	18	20	41	49	1							
32	01	17	23	34	37	49	1							
33	02	12	32	34	38	48	1							
34	09	19	31	35	39	42	1							
35	11	17	18	28	31	46	0							
36	03	08	16	20	24	25	2							
37	09	39	40	43	46	48	1							
38	05	08	12	15	39	47	2							
39	09	19	26	29	39	45	1							
40	05	15	30	35	41	48	1							
41	01	26	30	32	39	47	1							
42	07	08	13	26	32	35	2							
43	12	13	17	34	40	47	0							
44	08	23	33	40	46	49	1							
45	03	13	14	17	20	42	1							
46	14	17	27	41	47	48	0							
47	01	10	25	27	30	36	1							
48	16	21	31	40	43	45	0							
49	02	09	11	22	35	45	2							
50	03	11	32	34	44	48	1							
51	08	17	30	36	40	47	1							
52	07	13	16	24	35	42	1							

CHART 23

UK 2007 SATURDAY RESULTS
ANALYSIS OF LOTTERY NUMBERS IN THE TENS SERIES

WEEK No.	LOTTERY NUMBERS DRAWN						TOTAL IN WEEK	NUMBER OF TIMES PER WEEK IN YEAR						
								0	1	2	3	4	5	6
1	15	25	29	35	39	40	1	X	X	X	X	X		
2	05	08	12	20	28	48	1	X	X	X	X			
3	04	07	26	28	39	49	0	X	X	X	X			
4	04	15	21	23	24	38	1	X	X	X	X			
5	13	17	39	46	47	49	2	X	X	X	X			
6	22	26	38	39	41	42	0	X	X	X				
7	06	18	40	43	47	49	1	X	X	X				
8	05	18	26	34	42	49	1		X	X				
9	01	05	11	19	28	36	2		X	X				
10	01	09	16	34	38	41	1		X	X				
11	01	09	14	20	43	44	1		X	X				
12	09	14	26	28	30	45	1		X	X				
13	03	35	39	42	44	48	0		X					
14	23	24	30	31	33	37	0		X					
15	13	16	23	29	36	49	2		X					
16	14	20	21	30	41	46	1		X					
17	11	17	24	28	41	47	2		X					
18	04	33	34	38	39	49	0		X					
19	03	06	09	12	40	43	1		X					
20	17	19	20	32	36	48	2		X					
21	03	15	19	24	28	34	2		X					
22	01	10	33	35	38	43	1		X					
23	02	03	23	33	40	46	0		X					
24	08	17	33	41	43	45	1		X					
25	06	12	19	25	31	41	2		X					
26	10	11	17	34	38	46	3		X					
27	16	22	28	30	33	35	1		X					
28	15	27	35	37	38	39	1	7	27	12	5	1	0	0
29	03	10	21	25	29	49	1							
30	04	18	22	27	44	48	1							
31	12	23	25	26	34	49	1							
32	06	10	11	19	22	46	3							
33	02	12	26	32	37	47	1							
34	07	13	17	33	40	42	2							
35	03	27	34	41	42	48	0							
36	04	10	20	24	39	49	1							
37	03	07	12	21	25	36	1							
38	03	12	15	18	30	31	3							
39	01	09	10	11	16	49	3							
40	05	06	18	22	24	38	1							
41	07	11	12	36	38	39	2							
42	04	15	25	27	33	40	1							
43	06	08	10	13	22	32	2							
44	03	10	22	25	31	49	1							
45	05	11	13	18	25	35	3							
46	11	16	20	22	27	46	2							
47	01	14	25	37	39	47	1							
48	12	24	33	36	39	42	1							
49	04	06	10	11	24	33	2							
50	12	22	25	43	46	49	1							
51	11	13	14	16	21	44	4							
52	04	13	23	28	30	32	1							

Chapter 15

Considering Numbers in the Tens and Twenties Series (And Thirties and Forties)

MOVING on to Chart 23, the familiar chart of the 2007 U.K. Lottery results. This time, the numbers analysed are in the tens series: 10 through 19. Please note that there is one more number present than in the units series. The units series holds nine numbers and the tens series holds ten. This will affect the results.

Because there is one more number to select, the chances of them being selected increases. The analysis on the chart confirms this. There are many more weeks where three numbers in the tens series were drawn. There was even one week (week 51) where four numbers in the tens series (11, 13, 14, and 16) were drawn. This leads us to a possible policy of *ensuring that five or six of our future lottery numbers in any given selection are not in the tens series.*

But, of course we'll have to first check with the 2007 Canadian Lotto draw in order to be sure of the policy. For this, we review Chart 24 *(next page)*, which provides confirmation that it would be folly to have five or six lottery number selections present in one line that belong to the tens series.

In this particular chart, it is worthwhile noting that there are forty-two weeks where there were one or two numbers present in the tens series. So it would probably be worthwhile to include one or two numbers

47

CHART 24

CANADIAN LOTTO RESULTS 2007
ANALYSIS OF LOTTERY NUMBERS IN THE TENS' SERIES

WEEK No.	LOTTERY NUMBERS DRAWN						TOTAL IN WEEK	NUMBER OF TIMES PER WEEK IN YEAR						
								0	1	2	3	4	5	6
1	19	20	33	43	45	47	1	X	X	X	X			
2	01	02	03	19	25	41	1	X	X	X	X			
3	24	40	45	47	48	49	0	X	X	X	X			
4	06	09	17	20	22	40	1	X	X	X				
5	10	13	24	27	37	39	2	X	X	X				
6	08	13	23	37	41	42	1	X	X	X				
7	13	20	31	36	43	46	1	X	X	X				
8	04	06	15	33	38	40	1		X	X				
9	03	21	27	37	43	44	0		X	X				
10	09	18	28	37	42	49	1		X					
11	13	21	23	27	28	34	1		X					
12	01	13	19	26	32	46	2		X					
13	04	09	16	32	37	41	1		X					
14	10	12	23	26	35	37	2		X					
15	06	15	22	26	41	49	1		X					
16	17	29	33	43	45	49	1		X					
17	03	19	20	23	35	38	1		X					
18	01	23	26	28	33	40	0		X					
19	05	07	13	27	45	47	1		X					
20	08	16	33	37	40	42	1		X					
21	06	17	29	32	36	47	1		X					
22	08	16	19	32	40	46	2		X					
23	10	20	25	41	44	46	1		X					
24	03	15	31	33	43	48	1		X					
25	07	20	24	37	43	49	0		X					
26	06	12	25	43	45	47	1		X					
27	10	19	25	31	37	40	2		X					
28	10	27	33	38	40	49	1		X					
29	09	10	22	29	38	41	1		X					
30	01	05	17	32	39	45	1		X					
31	09	17	18	20	41	49	2		X					
32	01	17	23	34	37	49	1		X					
33	02	12	32	34	38	48	1		X					
34	09	19	31	35	39	42	1	7	33	9	3	0	0	0
35	11	17	18	28	31	46	3							
36	03	08	16	20	24	25	1							
37	09	39	40	43	46	48	0							
38	05	08	12	15	39	47	2							
39	09	19	26	29	39	45	1							
40	05	15	30	35	41	48	1							
41	01	26	30	32	39	47	0							
42	07	08	13	26	32	35	1							
43	12	13	17	34	40	47	3							
44	08	23	33	40	46	49	0							
45	03	13	14	17	20	42	3							
46	14	17	27	41	47	48	2							
47	01	10	25	27	30	36	1							
48	16	21	31	40	43	45	1							
49	02	09	11	22	35	45	1							
50	03	11	32	34	44	48	1							
51	08	17	30	36	40	47	1							
52	07	13	16	24	35	42	2							

CHART 25

UK 2007 SATURDAY RESULTS
ANALYSIS OF LOTTERY NUMBERS IN THE TWENTIES SERIES

WEEK No.	LOTTERY NUMBERS DRAWN						TOTAL IN WEEK	NUMBER OF TIMES PER WEEK IN YEAR						
								0	1	2	3	4	5	6
1	15	25	29	35	39	40	2	X	X	X	X			
2	05	08	12	20	28	48	2	X	X	X	X			
3	04	07	26	28	39	49	2	X	X	X	X			
4	04	15	21	23	24	38	3	X	X	X	X			
5	13	17	39	46	47	49	0	X	X	X				
6	22	26	38	39	41	42	2	X	X	X				
7	06	18	40	43	47	49	0	X	X	X				
8	05	18	26	34	42	49	1	X	X	X				
9	01	05	11	19	28	36	1	X	X	X				
10	01	09	16	34	38	41	0	X	X	X				
11	01	09	14	20	43	44	1	X	X	X				
12	09	14	26	28	30	45	2	X	X	X				
13	03	35	39	42	44	48	0	X	X	X				
14	23	24	30	31	33	37	2		X	X				
15	13	16	23	29	36	49	2		X	X				
16	14	20	21	30	41	46	2		X	X				
17	11	17	24	28	41	47	2			X				
18	04	33	34	38	39	49	0			X				
19	03	06	09	12	40	43	0			X				
20	17	19	20	32	36	48	1	13	16	19	4	0	0	0
21	03	15	19	24	28	34	2							
22	01	10	33	35	38	43	0							
23	02	03	23	33	40	46	1							
24	08	17	33	41	43	45	0							
25	06	12	19	25	31	41	1							
26	10	11	17	34	38	46	0							
27	16	22	28	30	33	35	2							
28	15	27	35	37	38	39	1							
29	03	10	21	25	29	49	3							
30	04	18	22	27	44	48	2							
31	12	23	25	26	34	49	3							
32	06	10	11	19	22	46	1							
33	02	12	26	32	37	47	1							
34	07	13	17	33	40	42	0							
35	03	27	34	41	42	48	1							
36	04	10	20	24	39	49	2							
37	03	07	12	21	25	36	2							
38	03	12	15	18	30	31	0							
39	01	09	10	11	16	49	0							
40	05	06	18	22	24	38	2							
41	07	11	12	36	38	39	0							
42	04	15	25	27	33	40	2							
43	06	08	10	13	22	32	1							
44	03	10	22	25	31	49	2							
45	05	11	13	18	25	35	1							
46	11	16	20	22	27	46	3							
47	01	14	25	37	39	47	1							
48	12	24	33	36	39	42	1							
49	04	06	10	11	24	33	1							
50	12	22	25	43	46	49	2							
51	11	13	14	16	21	44	1							
52	04	13	23	28	30	32	2							

of your selection in the tens series. But this is never the thrust of our argument as we are dealing with a mere vague suggestion. The main point we have proven is that *when choosing a line of future lottery numbers always ensure that 5 or 6 of them do not feature in the tens' series.*

As the twenties series also holds ten numbers, this would imply that one could select four numbers from the twenties series and be safe as well. Let's look at Chart 25 *(previous page)*. Recall that in week 51 of the 2007 U.K. National Lottery, there were four numbers in the twenties series present. There is always a doubt of where to draw the line in matters of creating a viable policy, but I bank on safety, which means that I would disallow four numbers in the twenties series to be present. But hey, let's see what the 2007 Canadian Lotto results have to say. Once this has been established, we might be in a position to create a policy for numbers in the thirties and forties series.

You might be thinking that examination of the frequency of numbers between 15 and 24 should be examined but, while you are quite correct, I am not going to do that. I have chosen to examine only the tens, twenties, thirties, and forties because it is very easy for me to do and for you to apply. Besides, the intermediate range from 15 to 24 is covered by the standard deviation examination that comes later. And, yes, the tens, twenties, thirties, and forties are also covered by the standard deviation test, but it is very difficult for you to do whereas this test is very easy. (I hope that hasn't confused you too much.) In the final analysis, all you really need do is take notice of the bold and italicized policy at the end of each section.

Let's have a look at Chart 26. Just as we thought, this chart confirms our suspicions. Week 11 of the 2007 Canadian Lotto has the following numbers drawn: 13, 21, 23, 27, 28, and 34. This selection is well within the realms of possibility that a line with four numbers from the twenties series could be drawn. Our policy is then quite clear. *When choosing a line of future lottery numbers, ensure that five or six of them do not feature in the twenties series.*

As there is the same number of numbers in the thirties and forties series, we can adopt a similar policy for those series. But be cautioned! I have spotted a line of five numbers in the forties series in the Canadian Lotto results. It occurred on week 3 and the results were 24, 40, 45, 47, 48, and 49. I judge this as a freak result, as it is very rare for all those series that have ten numbers within it. I believe it safe to say, that *when choosing a line of future lottery numbers, ensure that five or six of them are not in the thirties or forties series.*

CHART 26

CANADIAN LOTTO RESULTS 2007
ANALYSIS OF LOTTERY NUMBERS IN THE TWENTIES SERIES

WEEK No.	LOTTERY NUMBERS DRAWN						TOTAL IN WEEK	NUMBER OF TIMES PER WEEK IN YEAR						
								0	1	2	3	4	5	6
1	19	[20]	33	43	45	47	1	X	X	X	X	X		
2	01	02	03	19	[25]	41	1	X	X	X	X			
3	[24]	40	45	47	48	49	1	X	X	X				
4	06	09	17	[20]	[22]	40	2	X	X	X				
5	10	13	[24]	[27]	37	39	2	X	X	X				
6	08	13	[23]	37	41	42	1	X	X	X				
7	13	[20]	31	36	43	46	1	X	X	X				
8	04	06	15	33	38	40	0	X	X	X				
9	03	[21]	[27]	37	43	44	2	X	X	X				
10	09	18	[28]	37	42	49	1	X	X	X				
11	13	[21]	[23]	[27]	[28]	34	4	X	X	X				
12	01	13	19	[26]	32	46	1	X	X					
13	04	09	16	32	37	41	0	X	X					
14	10	12	[23]	[26]	35	37	2	X	X					
15	06	15	[22]	[26]	41	49	2		X					
16	17	[29]	33	43	45	49	1		X					
17	03	19	[20]	[23]	35	38	2		X					
18	01	[23]	[26]	[28]	33	40	3		X					
19	05	07	13	[27]	45	47	1		X					
20	08	16	33	37	40	42	0		X					
21	06	17	[29]	32	36	47	1		X					
22	08	16	19	32	40	46	0		X					
23	10	[20]	[25]	41	44	46	2		X					
24	03	15	31	33	43	48	0		X					
25	07	[20]	[24]	37	43	49	2	14	24	11	2	1	0	0
26	06	12	[25]	43	45	47	1							
27	10	19	[25]	31	37	40	1							
28	10	[27]	33	38	40	49	1							
29	09	10	[22]	[29]	38	41	2							
30	01	05	17	32	39	45	0							
31	09	17	18	[20]	41	49	1							
32	01	17	[23]	34	37	49	1							
33	02	12	32	34	38	48	0							
34	09	19	31	35	39	42	0							
35	11	17	18	[28]	31	46	1							
36	03	08	16	[20]	[24]	[25]	3							
37	09	39	40	43	46	48	0							
38	05	08	12	15	39	47	0							
39	09	19	[26]	[29]	39	45	2							
40	05	15	30	35	41	48	0							
41	01	[26]	30	32	39	47	1							
42	07	08	13	[26]	32	35	1							
43	12	13	17	34	40	47	0							
44	08	[23]	33	40	46	49	1							
45	03	13	14	17	[20]	42	1							
46	14	17	[27]	41	47	48	1							
47	01	10	[25]	[27]	30	36	2							
48	16	[21]	31	40	43	45	1							
49	02	09	11	[22]	35	45	1							
50	03	11	32	34	44	48	0							
51	08	17	30	36	40	47	0							
52	07	13	16	[24]	35	42	1							

51

Chapter 16

Considering the Primary Numbers

I'LL be asking you to have a look at the Chart 27 shortly. The type of number I'm going to examine this time are the primary numbers, those that can only be divided by themselves and 1.

But, before we go any farther, I have to say that the next few pages are really for pure academic purposes and have only a passing reference to the lottery. Feel free to skip directly to the page showing Chart 27.

Now this is very odd! There are two odd things here, in fact. (Frivolously I can say that the number 2 is a very odd prime indeed because its even!) The main odd feature is that the chart shows that the analysis works even though there seems to be no set sequence with primes. About one third of the numbers in the lottery are prime. They are 1, 2, 3, 5, 7, 11, 13, 17, 19, 23, 29, 31, 37, 41, 43, and 47. That's sixteen in all, about one third of the forty-nine numbers.

I include 1 as a prime number because it features the three main criteria for being one: it is divisible by itself and 1 only, every even number is produced by adding two primes together. (2 = 1+1), and it is produced when the routine opposite is evoked, as are all other primes.

It is merely by convention that most mathematicians disregard 1 as a prime number. They are simply wrong. There is an obscure logic to their reasoning, which, mercifully, has no bearing on reality either in mathematics or in our analysis here.

Recall that the whole basis of this book is to detect and discard order and sequences in lottery selections so that we have only truly random selections. Randomly and chaotically selected groups of numbers are what we require to mimic the draw! Mathematicians have never succeeded in finding a formula for producing primes and it was believed that none existed. They have achieved formulas of sorts, but their results weren't perfect. In addition to producing primes, these formulas produced composite numbers, which were called pseudo-primes. The main error that confounded these mathematicians was presuming that primes appeared to occur in a totally random fashion. But mathematicians Gauss and Riemann indicated that there could be order. I have found that order! So, why does the examination of primes in the lottery draw work well? Well, those mathematicians missed a little formula/routine/algorithm for checking whether or not numbers are prime.

It is: If (N! - N) modulus (N+1) = 0, then (N+1) = prime. N is the number with which you begin.

! is a mathematical function called factorial, which multiplies all the numbers listed from 1 up to N.

For example:
$4! = 1 \times 2 \times 3 \times 4 = 24$
$5! = 1 \times 2 \times 3 \times 4 \times 5 = 120$
$6! = 1 \times 2 \times 3 \times 4 \times 5 \times 6 = 720$

Modulus simply means the whole number left after division. Take, for example, N being equal to 5. Is (5 +1) prime? (i.e. 6) Then (120 - 5) = 115, 115/6 = 19 remainder 1. Therefore, 6 is not prime.

Take another example of N equalling 6. Is (6 + 1) prime? (i.e. 7) Then (720 - 6) = 714, 714/7 = 102 with no remainder left. Therefore 7 is a prime number.

Take another example of N equalling 12. Is (12 + 1) prime? (i.e. 13) Then, (4790011600 - 12) = 479001566, 479001566/13 = 36846276 with no remainder left. Therefore 13 is a prime number.

Those of you who are adventurous enough might like to test the routine in a simple QuickBasic program:

```
CLS
For P = 1 to 1000
For F = 3 to P
If P Mod (F-1) = 0 then Goto 10
Next F
Print using "####";P;
10 Next P
```

The above routine actually gives all prime numbers between 1 and 1,000 in less than one second. It takes a very long time to do a list of very large numbers even by computer based on the above routine. (Incidentally, I have modified the above algorithm to produce any single prime number within a very short time frame. It involved finding a slick method for factorialising numbers.)

So, because prime numbers can be derived from a formula, then examining lottery results based on prime numbers is valid. But, I must add that despite the prerequisite of there needing to be a formula-derived sequence of numbers before we can examine it, there could be merit in examining groups of numbers that are derived without a formula.

My main point to you, however, is that you should judge the charts as presented by me with your own eyes and interpretation. Use your own common sense to verify the conclusions. I, however, maintain that the final conclusions shriek their obvious truths at you. Ignore them at your own peril!

As I said before, it is not essential to understand exactly what I have been writing in the last few pages. Suffice it to say that we can proceed as before in examining the U.K. National Lottery results and then comparing them with the 2007 Canadian Lotto results. If the comparison is similar, we can use this to help us choose our future lottery selections.

As about one-third of the available lottery numbers are prime, you would expect that, on average, within any weekly lottery draw results that one third of them would also be prime. This, in fact, is the case and Chart 27 confirms this.

For this chart, I have highlighted prime numbers within the 2007 U.K. Lottery results. Does this tell us something about the 2007 lottery numbers? Of course it does! As with other analysis throughout this book, there are three values to be gleaned from studying the curve. In eighteen weeks of the year, there were two prime numbers drawn. This implies that you might include two prime numbers into each line of your lottery selections in future. In forty-five weeks of that year, there was at least one prime number present. Okay, okay, I know—this advice is a bit on the vague side, but the next piece of advice is solid!

There were no weeks in that year where five or six of the numbers drawn were prime. So, *when choosing a line of future lottery numbers, ensure that five or six of them are not prime.*

Let's look at Chart 28 *(next page)* to be sure. Note that in week 2 of the Canadian Lotto, there appeared five prime numbers. You might consider this a freak result, being only one week in the two years analyzed. Statisticians quite cheerfully would accept that, knowing that statistics is not

CHART 27

UK 2007 SATURDAY RESULTS
ANALYSIS OF LOTTERY NUMBERS THAT ARE PRIME

WEEK No.	LOTTERY NUMBERS DRAWN						TOTAL IN WEEK	NUMBER OF TIMES PER WEEK IN YEAR						
								0	1	2	3	4	5	6
1	15	25	29	35	39	40	1	X	X	X	X	X		
2	05	08	12	20	28	48	1	X	X	X	X	X		
3	04	07	26	28	39	49	1	X	X	X	X			
4	04	15	21	23	24	38	1	X	X	X	X			
5	13	17	39	46	47	49	3	X	X	X	X			
6	22	26	38	39	41	42	1	X	X	X	X			
7	06	18	40	43	47	49	2	X	X	X	X			
8	05	18	26	34	42	49	1		X	X	X			
9	01	05	11	19	28	36	4		X	X	X			
10	01	09	16	34	38	41	2		X	X	X			
11	01	09	14	20	43	44	2		X	X				
12	09	14	26	28	30	45	0		X	X				
13	03	35	39	42	44	48	1		X	X				
14	23	24	30	31	33	37	3		X	X				
15	13	16	23	29	36	49	3		X	X				
16	14	20	21	30	41	46	1		X					
17	11	17	24	28	41	47	4		X					
18	04	33	34	38	39	49	0		X					
19	03	06	09	12	40	43	2	7	15	18	10	2	0	0
20	17	19	20	32	36	48	2							
21	03	15	19	24	28	34	2							
22	01	10	33	35	38	43	2							
23	02	03	23	33	40	46	3							
24	08	17	33	41	43	45	3							
25	06	12	19	25	31	41	3							
26	10	11	17	34	38	46	2							
27	16	22	28	30	33	35	0							
28	15	27	35	37	38	39	1							
29	03	10	21	25	29	49	2							
30	04	18	22	27	44	48	0							
31	12	23	25	26	34	49	1							
32	06	10	11	19	22	46	2							
33	02	12	26	32	37	47	3							
34	07	13	17	33	40	42	3							
35	03	27	34	41	42	48	2							
36	04	10	20	24	39	49	0							
37	03	07	12	21	25	36	2							
38	03	12	15	18	30	31	2							
39	01	09	10	11	16	49	2							
40	05	06	18	22	24	38	1							
41	07	11	12	36	38	39	2							
42	04	15	25	27	33	40	0							
43	06	08	10	13	22	32	1							
44	03	10	22	25	31	49	2							
45	05	11	13	18	25	35	3							
46	11	16	20	22	27	46	1							
47	01	14	25	37	39	47	3							
48	12	24	33	36	39	42	0							
49	04	06	10	11	24	33	1							
50	12	22	25	43	46	49	1							
51	11	13	14	16	21	44	2							
52	04	13	23	28	30	32	2							

CHART 28

CANADIAN LOTTO RESULTS 2007
ANALYSIS OF LOTTERY NUMBERS THAT ARE PRIME

WEEK No.	LOTTERY NUMBERS DRAWN						TOTAL IN WEEK	NUMBER OF TIMES PER WEEK IN YEAR						
								0	1	2	3	4	5	6
1	19	20	33	43	45	47	3	X	X	X	X	X	X	
2	01	02	03	19	25	41	5	X	X	X	X	X		
3	24	40	45	47	48	49	1		X	X	X	X		
4	06	09	17	20	22	40	1		X	X	X			
5	10	13	24	27	37	39	2		X	X	X			
6	08	13	23	37	41	42	4		X	X	X			
7	13	20	31	36	43	46	3		X	X	X			
8	04	06	15	33	38	40	0		X	X	X			
9	03	21	27	37	43	44	3		X	X	X			
10	09	18	28	37	42	49	1		X	X	X			
11	13	21	23	27	28	34	2		X	X	X			
12	01	13	19	26	32	46	3		X	X	X			
13	04	09	16	32	37	41	1		X	X	X			
14	10	12	23	26	35	37	2			X	X			
15	06	15	22	26	41	49	1			X	X			
16	17	29	33	43	45	49	3			X	X			
17	03	19	20	23	35	38	3			X				
18	01	23	26	28	33	40	2	2	13	17	16	3	1	-
19	05	07	13	27	45	47	4							
20	08	16	33	37	40	42	1							
21	06	17	29	32	36	47	3							
22	08	16	19	32	40	46	1							
23	10	20	25	41	44	46	1							
24	03	15	31	33	43	48	3							
25	07	20	24	37	43	49	3							
26	06	12	25	43	45	47	3							
27	10	19	25	31	37	40	3							
28	10	27	33	38	40	49	0							
29	09	10	22	29	38	41	2							
30	01	05	17	32	39	45	3							
31	09	17	18	20	41	49	2							
32	01	17	23	34	37	49	4							
33	02	12	32	34	38	48	1							
34	09	19	31	35	39	42	2							
35	11	17	18	28	31	46	3							
36	03	08	16	20	24	25	1							
37	09	39	40	43	46	48	1							
38	05	08	12	15	39	47	2							
39	09	19	26	29	39	45	2							
40	05	15	30	35	41	48	2							
41	01	26	30	32	39	47	2							
42	07	08	13	26	32	35	2							
43	12	13	17	34	40	47	3							
44	08	23	33	40	46	49	1							
45	03	13	14	17	20	42	3							
46	14	17	27	41	47	48	3							
47	01	10	25	27	30	36	1							
48	16	21	31	40	43	45	2							
49	02	09	11	22	35	45	2							
50	03	11	32	34	44	48	2							
51	08	17	30	36	40	47	2							
52	07	13	16	24	35	42	2							

an exact science. I would agree with them. So, quite happily, I adopt the following policy: *When choosing a line of future lottery numbers, ensure that five or six of them are not prime.*

Prime numbers

Numbers that are prime: 1, 2, 3, 5, 7, 11, 13, 17, 19, 23, 29, 31, 37, 41, 43, and 47.

It would not be acceptable to choose a line with the numbers 2, 7, 17, 18, 41, and 47, as it includes five prime numbers. Nor would a line such as 2, 7, 18, 40, 41, and 43 be acceptable, as there are four prime numbers within it.

Chapter 17

Considering The Endings

MOVING on to a different analysis. Have a look at Chart 30, where the 2007 U.K. Lottery is analyzed based on numbers ending in 1. There are five such numbers in our lottery choices: 1, 11, 21, 31, and 41. It is a type of Lucas number and has the formula of adding 10 to the previous number beginning at 1. This special sequence is worth examining because the final analysis obeys the law of averages. Let me show you.

The percentage of times that numbers ending in 1 occurs in the forty-nine-number group is 10.2 percent. Throughout the year, there are (excluding bonus numbers) 6 x 52 lottery numbers drawn. This equals 312. Now 10.2 percent of 312 equals 32. This means that you would expect to see about thirty-two numbers drawn that end in 1 in each year. In the 2007 U.K. Lottery, there were thirty-one numbers that end in 1 drawn. Not bad! The above analysis merely goes to show that we are still on the correct path. We should be completely satisfied that we have yet again demonstrated that the so-called law of averages is still operating satisfactorily, and that we are fully exploiting it to our advantage!

However, the vital piece of information shown in the Chart 29 is that there were no weeks where three, four, or five numbers ending in 1 occurred. It might be worth considering that we should *avoid future selections where three, four, or five numbers ending in 1 occur.* But we must now look at the 2007 Canadian Lotto chart in order to confirm this.

Have a look at Chart 30 *(next page)* to see how numbers ending in 1 occurred in the 2007 Canadian Lotto. There were twenty-seven weeks where no numbers ending in 1 were drawn. There were twenty-three weeks in

CHART 29

UK 2007 SATURDAY RESULTS
ANALYSIS OF LOTTERY NUMBERS ENDING IN '1'

WEEK No.	LOTTERY NUMBERS DRAWN						TOTAL IN WEEK	NUMBER OF TIMES PER WEEK IN YEAR						
								0	1	2	3	4	5	6
1	15	25	29	35	39	40	0	X	X	X				
2	05	08	12	20	28	48	0	X	X	X				
3	04	07	26	28	39	49	0	X	X	X				
4	04	15	[21]	23	24	38	1	X	X	X				
5	13	17	39	46	47	49	0	X	X	X				
6	22	26	38	39	[41]	42	1	X	X	X				
7	06	18	40	43	47	49	0	X	X	X				
8	05	18	26	34	42	49	0	X	X					
9	[01]	05	[11]	19	28	36	2	X	X					
10	[01]	09	16	34	38	[41]	2	X	X					
11	[01]	09	14	20	43	44	1	X	X					
12	09	14	26	28	30	45	0	X	X					
13	03	35	39	42	44	48	0	X	X					
14	23	24	30	[31]	33	37	1	X	X					
15	13	16	23	29	36	49	0	X	X					
16	14	20	[21]	30	[41]	46	2	X	X					
17	[11]	17	24	28	[41]	47	2	X	X					
18	04	33	34	38	39	49	0	X						
19	03	06	09	12	40	43	0	X						
20	17	19	20	32	36	48	0	X						
21	03	15	19	24	28	34	0	X						
22	[01]	10	33	35	38	43	1	X						
23	02	03	23	33	40	46	0	X						
24	08	17	33	[41]	43	45	1	X						
25	06	12	19	25	[31]	[41]	2	X						
26	10	[11]	17	34	38	46	1	X						
27	16	22	28	30	33	35	0	X						
28	15	27	35	37	38	39	0	X						
29	03	10	[21]	25	29	49	0	28	17	7	0	0	0	-
30	04	18	22	27	44	48	0							
31	12	23	25	26	34	49	0							
32	06	10	[11]	19	22	46	1							
33	02	12	26	32	37	47	0							
34	07	13	17	33	40	42	0							
35	03	27	34	[41]	42	48	1							
36	04	10	20	24	39	49	0							
37	03	07	12	[21]	25	36	1							
38	03	12	15	18	30	[31]	1							
39	[01]	09	10	[11]	16	49	2							
40	05	06	18	22	24	38	0							
41	07	[11]	12	36	38	39	1							
42	04	15	25	27	33	40	0							
43	06	08	10	13	22	32	0							
44	03	10	22	25	[31]	49	1							
45	05	[11]	13	18	25	35	1							
46	[11]	16	20	22	27	46	1							
47	[01]	14	25	37	39	47	1							
48	12	24	33	36	39	42	0							
49	04	06	10	[11]	24	33	1							
50	12	22	25	43	46	49	0							
51	[11]	13	14	16	[21]	44	2							
52	04	13	23	28	30	32	0							

CHART 30

CANADIAN LOTTO RESULTS 2007
ANALYSIS OF LOTTERY NUMBERS ENDING IN '1'

WEEK No.	LOTTERY NUMBERS DRAWN						TOTAL IN WEEK	NUMBER OF TIMES PER WEEK IN YEAR						
								0	1	2	3	4	5	6
1	19	20	33	43	45	47	0	X	X	X				
2	[01]	02	03	19	25	[41]	2	X	X	X				
3	24	40	45	47	48	49	0	X	X					
4	06	09	17	20	22	40	0	X	X					
5	10	13	24	27	37	39	0	X	X					
6	08	13	23	37	[41]	42	1	X	X					
7	13	20	[31]	36	43	46	1	X	X					
8	04	06	15	33	38	40	0	X	X					
9	03	[21]	27	37	43	44	1	X	X					
10	09	18	28	37	42	49	0	X	X					
11	13	[21]	23	27	28	34	1	X	X					
12	[01]	13	19	26	32	46	1	X	X					
13	04	09	16	32	37	[41]	1	X	X					
14	10	12	23	26	35	37	0	X	X					
15	06	15	22	26	[41]	49	1	X	X					
16	17	29	33	43	45	49	0	X	X					
17	03	19	20	23	35	38	0	X	X					
18	[01]	23	26	28	33	40	1	X	X					
19	05	07	13	27	45	47	0	X	X					
20	08	16	33	37	40	42	0	X	X					
21	06	17	29	32	36	47	0	X	X					
22	08	16	19	32	40	46	0	X	X					
23	10	20	25	[41]	44	46	1	X	X					
24	03	15	[31]	33	43	48	1	X						
25	07	20	24	37	43	49	0	X						
26	06	12	25	43	45	47	0	X						
27	10	19	25	[31]	37	40	1	X						
28	10	27	33	38	40	49	0	27	23	2	0	0	0	-
29	09	10	22	29	38	[41]	1							
30	[01]	05	17	32	39	45	1							
31	09	17	18	20	[41]	49	1							
32	[01]	17	23	34	37	49	1							
33	02	12	32	34	38	48	0							
34	09	19	[31]	35	39	42	1							
35	[11]	17	18	28	[31]	46	2							
36	03	08	16	20	24	25	0							
37	09	39	40	43	46	48	0							
38	05	08	12	15	39	47	0							
39	09	19	26	29	39	45	0							
40	05	15	30	35	[41]	48	1							
41	[01]	26	30	32	39	47	1							
42	07	08	13	26	32	35	0							
43	12	13	17	34	40	47	0							
44	08	23	33	40	46	49	0							
45	03	13	14	17	20	42	0							
46	14	17	27	[41]	47	48	1							
47	[01]	10	25	27	30	36	1							
48	16	[21]	31	40	43	45	1							
49	02	09	[11]	22	35	45	1							
50	03	[11]	32	34	44	48	1							
51	08	17	30	36	40	47	0							
52	07	13	16	24	35	42	0							

that year where there was one number ending in 1 present. There were two weeks where there were two numbers ending in 1 present. There were zero weeks in that year where there were three, four, or five numbers ending in 1 present. This last statement is different from the U.K. result and we therefore must take that into account when proposing the policy to adopt. This policy is, *when choosing a line of future lottery numbers, ensure that there are never three, four, or five of them ending in 1.*

You'll remember that I previously asked you to make a little leap in logic. Well, allow me to make the same request in order to spare you too much repeated explanation of the same idea. There are five numbers ending in 1. There are also five numbers that end in 2, 3, 4, 5, 6, 7, 8, and 9. (Numbers ending in 0 are dealt with in the division by 10s section.) Therefore, the same policy can be applied to these other endings. We can safely say that *when choosing a line of future lottery numbers, ensure that there are never three, four, or five of them ending in 2, 3, 4, 5, 6, 7, 8, or 9.*

Chapter 18

Considering the Sum Total

LET'S now have a look at Chart 31, where the 2007 U.K. Lottery results are added up on a weekly basis. For example, in week 1 the draw consisted of the numbers 15, 25, 29, 35, 39, and 40. These add up to 183. This value is placed in the *Weekly Total* column and an X is placed on the chart in the 165-to-193-range column. The rest of the year was totalled on a weekly basis and information entered in a similar fashion.

In week 49, the lottery numbers' total of 88 is highlighted. In weeks 5 and 13 the lottery numbers' total of 211 is also highlighted. These represent the lowest and highest weekly total values. These values indicate a policy: *When choosing a line of future lottery numbers, ensure that their sum never totals less than 88 or more than 211.*

For example, 1 + 2 + 4 + 7 + 8 + 9 totals 31. This is less than 88 and a very doubtful entry. It should be avoided. Another example considers the numbers 27, 30, 31, 37, 43, 48. These total 216 and, as an entry, it is doubtful and should also be avoided. Before we get carried away with premature advice, we'd better check the 2007 Canadian Lotto to see if it confirms what we suspect.

These results are shown in Chart 32 *(next page)*. There are two main things to note here. First, the lowest sum is 91 (you will find this in week 2) and, second, the highest total is 253 (found in week 3). Both these values are highlighted.

You will recall that the previous chart showed a minimum of 88 in week 1 and a maximum of 211 in weeks 5 and 13. So, to be absolute sure of the best policy to adopt, I think it would be wise to make the lowest

CHART 31

UK 2007 SATURDAY RESULTS
ANALYSIS OF LOTTERY NUMBERS BY WEEKLY ADDITION

WEEK No.	LOTTERY NUMBERS DRAWN						TOTAL IN WEEK	21 to 48	49 to 77	78 to 106	107 to 135	136 to 164	165 to 193	194 to 222	223 to 251	252 to 279
1	15	25	29	35	39	40	183			X	X	X	X	X		
2	05	08	12	20	28	48	121			X	X	X	X	X		
3	04	07	26	28	39	49	153			X	X	X	X	X		
4	04	15	21	23	24	38	125			X	X	X	X	X		
5	13	17	39	46	47	49	211			X	X	X	X	X		
6	22	26	38	39	41	42	208				X	X	X	X		
7	06	18	40	43	47	49	203				X	X	X	X		
8	05	18	26	34	42	49	174				X	X	X			
9	01	05	11	19	28	36	100				X	X	X			
10	01	09	16	34	38	41	139				X	X	X			
11	01	09	14	20	43	44	131				X	X	X			
12	09	14	26	28	30	45	152				X	X				
13	03	35	39	42	44	48	211					X				
14	23	24	30	31	33	37	178					X				
15	13	16	23	29	36	49	166					X				
16	14	20	21	30	41	46	172					X				
17	11	17	24	28	41	47	168					X				
18	04	33	34	38	39	49	197	0	0	5	12	17	11	7	0	0
19	03	06	09	12	40	43	113									
20	17	19	20	32	36	48	172									
21	03	15	19	24	28	34	123									
22	01	10	33	35	38	43	160									
23	02	03	23	33	40	46	147									
24	08	17	33	41	43	45	187									
25	06	12	19	25	31	41	134									
26	10	11	17	34	38	46	156									
27	16	22	28	30	33	35	164									
28	15	27	35	37	38	39	191									
29	03	10	21	25	29	49	137									
30	04	18	22	27	44	48	163									
31	12	23	25	26	34	49	169									
32	06	10	11	19	22	46	114									
33	02	12	26	32	37	47	156									
34	07	13	17	33	40	42	152									
35	03	27	34	41	42	48	195									
36	04	10	20	24	39	49	146									
37	03	07	12	21	25	36	104									
38	03	12	15	18	30	31	109									
39	01	09	10	11	16	49	96									
40	05	06	18	22	24	38	113									
41	07	11	12	36	38	39	143									
42	04	15	25	27	33	40	144									
43	06	08	10	13	22	32	91									
44	03	10	22	25	31	49	140									
45	05	11	13	18	25	35	107									
46	11	16	20	22	27	46	142									
47	01	14	25	37	39	47	163									
48	12	24	33	36	39	42	186									
49	04	06	10	11	24	33	88									
50	12	22	25	43	46	49	197									
51	11	13	14	16	21	44	119									
52	04	13	23	28	30	32	130									

THE WEEKLY AVERAGE IS -   151

CHART 32

CANADIAN LOTTO RESULTS 2007
ANALYSIS OF LOTTERY NUMBERS BY WEEKLY ADDITION

WEEK No.	LOTTERY NUMBERS DRAWN						TOTAL IN WEEK	ADDITION RANGE PER WEEK IN YEAR								
								21 to 48	49 to 77	78 to 106	107 to 135	136 to 164	165 to 193	194 to 222	223 to 251	252 to 279
1	19	20	33	43	45	47	207		X	X	X	X	X	X	X	X
2	01	02	03	19	25	41	91		X	X	X	X	X			
3	24	40	45	47	48	49	253			X	X	X	X			
4	06	09	17	20	22	40	114			X	X	X	X			
5	10	13	24	27	37	39	150			X	X	X	X			
6	08	13	23	37	41	42	164			X	X	X	X			
7	13	20	31	36	43	46	189					X	X			
8	04	06	15	33	38	40	136					X	X			
9	03	21	27	37	43	44	175					X	X			
10	09	18	28	37	42	49	183					X	X			
11	13	21	23	27	28	34	146					X	X			
12	01	13	19	26	32	46	137					X	X			
13	04	09	16	32	37	41	139					X	X			
14	10	12	23	26	35	37	143					X	X			
15	06	15	22	26	41	49	159					X	X			
16	17	29	33	43	45	49	216					X	X			
17	03	19	20	23	35	38	138					X				
18	01	23	26	28	33	40	151					X				
19	05	07	13	27	45	47	144					X				
20	08	16	33	37	40	42	176					X				
21	06	17	29	32	36	47	167	0	0	2	6	20	16	6	1	1
22	08	16	19	32	40	46	161									
23	10	20	25	41	44	46	186									
24	03	15	31	33	43	48	173									
25	07	20	24	37	43	49	180									
26	06	12	25	43	45	47	178									
27	10	19	25	31	37	40	162									
28	10	27	33	38	40	49	197									
29	09	10	22	29	38	41	149									
30	01	05	17	32	39	45	139									
31	09	17	18	20	41	49	154									
32	01	17	23	34	37	49	161									
33	02	12	32	34	38	48	166									
34	09	19	31	35	39	42	175									
35	11	17	18	28	31	46	151									
36	03	08	16	20	24	25	96									
37	09	39	40	43	46	48	225									
38	05	08	12	15	39	47	126									
39	09	19	26	29	39	45	167									
40	05	15	30	35	41	48	174									
41	01	26	30	32	39	47	175									
42	07	08	13	26	32	35	121									
43	12	13	17	34	40	47	163									
44	08	23	33	40	46	49	199									
45	03	13	14	17	20	42	109									
46	14	17	27	41	47	48	194									
47	01	10	25	27	30	36	129									
48	16	21	31	40	43	45	196									
49	02	09	11	22	35	45	124									
50	03	11	32	34	44	48	172									
51	08	17	30	36	40	47	178									
52	07	13	16	24	35	42	137									
	THE WEEKLY AVERAGE IS -						161									

acceptable number the lowest of the two lotteries. It would also be wise to make the highest acceptable total number the higher of the two lotteries. The best policy to be had out of this analysis is: ***When choosing a line of future lottery numbers, ensure that their sum never totals less than 82 or more than 253.***

For example, a line consisting of 1, 8, 10, 12, 23, and 27 equals 81, and so is unacceptable. Likewise, a line consisting of 30, 40, 43, 46, 47, and 48 equals 254 and is also unacceptable. However, a line consisting of 9, 12, 29, 32, 33, and 40 equals 155, which is acceptable.

From the right-hand portion of Chart 32, you can see that almost all of the winning numbers fall within the range of 107 to 222. It might be a good idea to confine your own selections to that range.

Chapter 19

Considering the
Standard Deviation

THERE is yet another obscure way of looking at sets of numbers, which I'm sure you never considered but at the same time could possibly help you to choose better selections of lottery numbers. It involves examining the standard deviation of sets of numbers. All scientific calculators have the capability to perform standard deviation calculations. Before I explain further, I would like to delve a little into the background of this side of mathematics. Fair warning: These next two pages are really for academic purposes only and there is just a passing reference to the lottery. Feel free to skip directly to Chart 33.

For simplicity's sake and clarity, I'm going to use numbers that feature only in the National Lottery (1 through 49). Consider these two sets of numbers: 1, 2, 3, 47, 48, and 49 and 1, 3, 24, 25, 47, and 49. The obvious things that we can observe about these two sets of numbers are:

- their averages are 24.5 each,
- their lowest number is 1, and
- their highest number is 49.

Both sets are clearly different from each other, but how can we describe the differences mathematically? There is so much similar with both sets that this seems to be an impossible task. What can we do arithmetically to the numbers to show the differences? Well, this problem was noticed by our good friend Karl Friedrich Gauss (1777–1855), the father of statistical reasoning whose curves you have been studying throughout this book. His system involved multiplying and squaring combinations of the numbers, subtracting one set from another, and finding the square root of those to leave a statistical value for each set. (Ouch!)

The verbal description of the first set of numbers is that these numbers are not close to the set average. (The average of 1 + 2 + 3 is not close to 24.5, neither is the average of 47 + 48 + 49.) The verbal description of the second set of numbers is that these numbers are closer to the set average. (The average of 1 + 3 + 24 is closer to 24.5 as is 25 + 47 + 49.)

The standard deviation of the first set of numbers works out at 25.2, while the standard deviation of the second set of numbers works out to 20.6 Actually, all *standard deviation* means is "the average value away from the set average." In layman's terms, one could say that an answer is "an average of X, give or take a few" (X being some value discussed).

If you have a statistical or scientific calculator, you can easily do this type of calculation yourself. You will have to engage the SD mode. This is one of the calculations done by my computer software program automatically, by the way.

This calculation is definitely worth doing if we are to get the edge over our fellow lottery punters and reduce the odds in our favor. The following pages examine the results and analysis of the U.K. and Canadian lotteries from the standard deviation point of view.

In Chart 33 (*next page*), the 2007 U.K. Lottery numbers were examined from the standard deviation point of view. The chart shows that yet another Gaussian-curve result from the analysis. As expected, we find a clutch of results in the middle and the extremities bare.

The lowest standard deviation was 5. In layman's terms, this simply means that the lottery results were grouped far too tightly together. The highest standard deviation value was 19, in other words, the lottery results were too wide apart. The bulk of the values fell between these two values. So we must conclude *that we should not consider lottery picks where the standard deviation is less than 5 or more than 19.*

So, do we have yet another policy beckoning? We probably do, but first let's see if the weekly standard deviation of the 2007 Canadian Lotto results bears out the above conclusion.

Chart 34 (*next page*) shows the standard deviation analysis of the Canadian Lotto results. Again, we find that there is merit in avoiding the extremities of any of the curves printed in this book. The same goes for the standard deviation curves. We already know that in the 2007 U.K. Lottery analysis, a value of less than 5 is bad and should be avoided. A value of more than 20 is also bad and should be avoided. The values occurring between are acceptable.

CHART 33

UK 2007 SATURDAY RESULTS
ANALYSIS OF LOTTERY NUMBERS BY THEIR WEEKLY STANDARD DEVIATION

WEEK No.	LOTTERY NUMBERS DRAWN	WEEKLY S.D.	2 to 4	5 to 7	8 to 10	11 to 13	14 to 16	17 to 19	20 to 22	23 to 25
1	15 25 29 35 39 40	10		X	X	X	X	X		
2	05 08 12 20 28 48	16		X	X	X	X	X		
3	04 07 26 28 39 49	15			X	X	X	X		
4	04 15 21 23 24 38	11			X	X	X	X		
5	13 17 39 46 47 49	16				X	X	X		
6	22 26 38 39 41 42	08				X	X	X		
7	06 18 40 43 47 49	18				X	X	X		
8	05 18 26 34 42 49	16				X	X	X		
9	01 05 11 19 28 36	14				X	X	X		
10	01 09 16 34 38 41	17				X	X	X		
11	01 09 14 20 43 44	18				X	X			
12	09 14 26 28 30 45	13				X	X			
13	03 35 39 42 44 48	16				X	X			
14	23 24 30 31 33 37	05				X	X			
15	13 16 23 29 36 49	13				X	X			
16	14 20 21 30 41 46	13				X	X			
17	11 17 24 28 41 47	14				X	X			
18	04 33 34 38 39 49	15				X				
19	03 06 09 12 40 43	18				X				
20	17 19 20 32 36 48	12	0	2	4	18	18	10	0	0
21	03 15 19 24 28 34	11								
22	01 10 33 35 38 43	17								
23	02 03 23 33 40 46	19								
24	08 17 33 41 43 45	15								
25	06 12 19 25 31 41	13								
26	10 11 17 34 38 46	15								
27	16 22 28 30 33 35	07								
28	15 27 35 37 38 39	10								
29	03 10 21 25 29 49	16								
30	04 18 22 27 44 48	17								
31	12 23 25 26 34 49	12								
32	06 10 11 19 22 46	15								
33	02 12 26 32 37 47	17								
34	07 13 17 33 40 42	15								
35	03 27 34 41 42 48	16								
36	04 10 20 24 39 49	16								
37	03 07 12 21 25 36	12								
38	03 12 15 18 30 31	11								
39	01 09 10 11 16 49	17								
40	05 06 18 22 24 38	12								
41	07 11 12 36 38 39	15								
42	04 15 25 27 33 40	13								
43	06 08 10 13 22 32	10								
44	03 10 22 25 31 49	16								
45	05 11 13 18 25 35	11								
46	11 16 20 22 27 46	12								
47	01 14 25 37 39 47	17								
48	12 24 33 36 39 42	11								
49	04 06 10 11 24 33	11								
50	12 22 25 43 46 49	15								
51	11 13 14 16 21 44	12								
52	04 13 23 28 30 32	11								

CHART 34

CANADIAN LOTTO RESULTS 2007
ANALYSIS OF LOTTERY NUMBERS BY THEIR WEEKLY STANDARD DEVIATION

WEEK No.	LOTTERY NUMBERS DRAWN						WEEKLY S.D.	RANGES OF S.D. PER WEEK IN YEAR							
								2 to 4	5 to 7	8 to 10	11 to 13	14 to 16	17 to 19	20 to 22	23 to 25
1	15	25	29	35	39	40	10		X	X	X	X	X	X	
2	05	08	12	20	28	48	16		X	X	X	X	X		
3	04	07	26	28	39	49	18			X	X	X	X		
4	04	15	21	23	24	38	11			X	X	X	X		
5	13	17	39	46	47	49	16				X	X	X		
6	22	26	38	39	41	42	08				X	X	X		
7	06	18	40	43	47	49	18				X	X	X		
8	05	18	26	34	42	49	16				X	X	X		
9	01	05	11	19	28	36	14				X	X	X		
10	01	09	16	34	38	41	17				X	X	X		
11	01	09	14	20	43	44	18				X	X	X		
12	09	14	26	28	30	45	13				X	X	X		
13	03	35	39	42	44	48	20				X	X			
14	23	24	30	31	33	37	05				X	X			
15	13	16	23	29	36	49	13				X	X			
16	14	20	21	30	41	46	13				X				
17	11	17	24	28	41	47	14				X				
18	04	33	34	38	39	49	15				X				
19	03	06	09	12	40	43	18	0	2	4	18	15	12	1	0
20	17	19	20	32	36	48	12								
21	03	15	19	24	28	34	11								
22	01	10	33	35	38	43	17								
23	02	03	23	33	40	46	19								
24	08	17	33	41	43	45	15								
25	06	12	19	25	31	41	13								
26	10	11	17	34	38	46	15								
27	16	22	28	30	33	35	07								
28	15	27	35	37	38	39	09								
29	03	10	21	25	29	49	16								
30	04	18	22	27	44	48	17								
31	12	23	25	26	34	49	12								
32	06	10	11	19	22	46	15								
33	02	12	26	32	37	47	17								
34	07	13	17	33	40	42	15								
35	03	27	34	41	42	48	16								
36	04	10	20	24	39	49	17								
37	03	07	12	21	25	36	12								
38	03	12	15	18	30	31	11								
39	01	09	10	11	16	49	17								
40	05	06	18	22	24	38	12								
41	07	11	12	36	38	39	15								
42	04	15	25	27	33	40	13								
43	06	08	10	13	22	32	10								
44	03	10	22	25	31	49	16								
45	05	11	13	18	25	35	11								
46	11	16	20	22	27	46	12								
47	01	14	25	37	39	47	17								
48	12	24	33	36	39	42	11								
49	04	06	10	11	24	33	11								
50	12	22	25	43	46	49	15								
51	11	13	14	16	21	44	12								
52	04	13	23	28	30	32	11								

The extreme values in Chart 34 are 5 and 20. (I have ringed them for clarity.) The extreme values in Chart 33 were 5 and 19. It is logical to use the lowest and highest values of both to form our policy. Therefore, we can say that *when choosing a line of future lottery numbers, ensure that the standard deviation value of the set is never less than 5 or more than 20.*

An example of a set with very low standard deviation is: 17, 18, 20, 22, 23, 27. The standard deviation of this set is 4, which is way too low. The numbers are grouped far too tightly together.

An example of a set with very high standard deviation is: 4, 9, 38, 44, 49. The standard deviation here is 22, far too high. The numbers are too wide apart.

Chapter 20

Considering the Highs and Lows

WHEN the Lottery results are announced on the television immediately after the draw, they are then displayed visually in numerically ascending order. What I have done to in Chart 35 *(next page)* is ring the lowest and highest U.K. 2007 Lottery number in each column. The idea is that if we find the range of the values of each lottery position, then we could confine our selections to match.

In the first column, the lowest number is 1 and the highest number is 23. In the second column, the lowest number is 3 and the highest number is 35. In the third column the lowest is 9 and the highest is 40. In the fourth column, 12 and 46. In the fifth column, 16 and 47. In the sixth column, the 31 and 49.

The procedure to take advantage of this view is to first select a line of lottery numbers, arrange them in ascending order etc, etc . . . For example, 43, 12, 47, 32, 13, and 4 becomes 4, 12, 13, 32, 43, and 47.

You then do the following checks:

- Check that the first number is between 1 and 26 (4 is okay)
- Check that the second number is between 3 and 35 (12 is okay)
- Check that the third number is between 9 and 40 (13 is okay)
- Check that the fourth number is between 12 and 46 (32 is okay)
- Check that the fifth number is between 16 and 47 (43 is okay)
- Check that the sixth number is between 31 and 49 (47 is okay)

CHART 35

UK 2007 SATURDAY RESULTS
ANALYSIS OF LOTTERY NUMBERS BY
LOWEST AND HIGHEST IN EACH COLUMN

WEEK No.	LOTTERY NUMBERS DRAWN					
1	15	25	29	35	39	40
2	05	08	12	20	28	48
3	04	07	26	28	39	49
4	04	15	21	23	24	38
5	13	17	39	46	47	49
6	22	26	38	39	41	42
7	06	18	40	43	47	49
8	05	18	26	34	42	49
9	01	05	11	19	28	36
10	01	09	16	34	38	41
11	01	09	14	20	43	44
12	09	14	26	28	30	45
13	03	35	39	42	44	48
14	23	24	30	31	33	37
15	13	16	23	29	36	49
16	14	20	21	30	41	46
17	11	17	24	28	41	47
18	04	33	34	38	39	49
19	03	06	09	12	40	43
20	17	19	20	32	36	48
21	03	15	19	24	28	34
22	01	10	33	35	38	43
23	02	03	23	33	40	46
24	08	17	33	41	43	45
25	06	12	19	25	31	41
26	10	11	17	34	38	46
27	16	22	28	30	33	35
28	15	27	35	37	38	39
29	03	10	21	25	29	49
30	04	18	22	27	44	48
31	12	23	25	26	34	49
32	06	10	11	19	22	46
33	02	12	26	32	37	47
34	07	13	17	33	40	42
35	03	27	34	41	42	48
36	04	10	20	24	39	49
37	03	07	12	21	25	36
38	03	12	15	18	30	31
39	01	09	10	11	16	49
40	05	06	18	22	24	38
41	07	11	12	36	38	39
42	04	15	25	27	33	40
43	06	08	10	13	22	32
44	03	10	22	25	31	49
45	05	11	13	18	25	35
46	11	16	20	22	27	46
47	01	14	25	37	39	47
48	12	24	33	36	39	42
49	04	06	10	11	24	33
50	12	22	25	43	46	49
51	11	13	14	16	21	44
52	04	13	23	28	30	32

This sounds like a very reasonable check to do with your numbers, but before we adopt the above as a firm policy we'd better check with the 2007 Canadian Lotto analyzed in Chart 36 to see if the numbers agree.

On this chart, I have marked up the lowest and highest numbers of each column after listing the 2007 Canadian Lotto results.

In the first column the lowest number is 1 and the highest number is 24. In the second column, the lowest is 2 and the highest is 40. In the third column, 3 and 45. In the fourth column, 15 and 47. In the fifth column, 16 and 48. In the sixth column, 25 and 49.

The above list is slightly different from the U.K. Lottery results. To ensure as safe as possible a policy to adopt, it is best that the lowest number from either chart and the highest number from either chart employed. This gives us the following policies:

- *When choosing a line of future lottery numbers, ensure that the first number is within the range of 1 through 24.*

72

CHART 36

CANADIAN LOTTO RESULTS 2007
ANALYSIS OF LOTTERY NUMBERS BY
LOWEST AND HIGHEST IN EACH COLUMN

WEEK No.	LOTTERY NUMBERS DRAWN					
1	19	20	33	43	45	47
2	01	02	03	19	25	41
3	24	40	45	47	48	49
4	06	09	17	20	22	40
5	10	13	24	27	37	39
6	08	13	23	37	41	42
7	13	20	31	36	43	46
8	04	06	15	33	38	40
9	03	21	27	37	43	44
10	09	18	28	37	42	49
11	13	21	23	27	28	34
12	01	13	19	26	32	46
13	04	09	16	32	37	41
14	10	12	23	26	35	37
15	06	15	22	26	41	49
16	17	29	33	43	45	49
17	03	19	20	23	35	38
18	01	23	26	28	33	40
19	05	07	13	27	45	47
20	08	16	33	37	40	42
21	06	17	29	32	36	47
22	08	16	19	32	40	46
23	10	20	25	41	44	46
24	03	15	31	33	43	48
25	07	20	24	37	43	49
26	06	12	25	43	45	47
27	10	19	25	31	37	40
28	10	27	33	38	40	49
29	09	10	22	29	38	41
30	01	05	17	32	39	45
31	09	17	18	20	41	49
32	01	17	23	34	37	49
33	02	12	32	34	38	48
34	09	19	31	35	39	42
35	11	17	18	28	31	46
36	03	08	16	20	24	25
37	09	39	40	43	46	48
38	05	08	12	15	39	47
39	09	19	26	29	39	45
40	05	15	30	35	41	48
41	01	26	30	32	39	47
42	07	08	13	26	32	35
43	12	13	17	34	40	47
44	08	23	33	40	46	49
45	03	13	14	17	20	42
46	14	17	27	41	47	48
47	01	10	25	27	30	36
48	16	21	31	40	43	45
49	02	09	11	22	35	45
50	03	11	32	34	44	48
51	08	17	30	36	40	47
52	07	13	16	24	35	42

- *When choosing a line of future lottery numbers, ensure that the second number is within the range of 2 through 40.*

- *When choosing a line of future lottery numbers, ensure that the third number is within the range of 3 through 45.*

- *When choosing a line of future lottery numbers, ensure that the fourth number is within the range of 12 through 47.*

- *When choosing a line of future lottery numbers, ensure that the fifth number is within the range of 14 through 48.*

- *When choosing a line of future lottery numbers, ensure that the sixth number is within the range of 25 through 49.*

If you choose 8, 11, 19, 20, 23, and 24, then the last number would not be acceptable as it is not with the range of 25 through 49.

Chapter 21

Considering the Degree of Separation; What's the Difference?

HAVE you noticed that in most weeks' lottery results, there are two numbers close together? The separation is either by 1, such as 17 and 18 or by 2, such as 34, and 36. Have a look at Chart 37. I analysed all the differences between the numbers in both U.K. and Canadian lotteries. There's a point to bear in mind here: To calculate the differences between the numbers is easy enough until you wish to find the difference between the first number and the last. I did this by counting the position in a clockwise fashion from the sixth number to the first (having placed the forty-nine numbers in a clockwise circle first). So, if 2 and 48 were the first and last numbers of a lottery draw, the difference between them would be 3 and not 46. You can view this the same way as you would view the difference between 10:00 a.m. and 1:00 p.m. The obvious difference between the two times is 3 hours, not 9.

There is a second point to note: After I calculated the differences, I placed these differences in ascending order. This would allow me to make a meaningful analysis of the table of results. Let me illustrate:

In week 1 of the 2007 U.K. lottery, the draw was 15, 25, 29, 35, 39, and 40. The difference between 15 and 25 is 10. The difference between 25 and 29 is 4. The difference between 29 and 35 is 6. The difference between 35 and 39 is 4. The difference between 39 and 40 is 1. The difference between 40 and 15 is 24 (not 25).

CHART 37

UK 2007 SATURDAY RESULTS
ANALYSIS OF THE DIFFERENCES BETWEEN LOTTERY NUMBERS DRAWN
THEN PLACED IN ASCENDING ORDER

WEEK No.	LOTTERY NUMBERS						DIFFERENCES BETWEEN WHEN PLACED IN ASCENDING ORDER					
1	15	25	29	35	39	40	[1]	4	4	6	10	24
2	05	08	12	20	28	48	3	4	6	8	8	20
3	04	07	26	28	39	49	2	3	4	10	11	19
4	04	15	21	23	24	38	1	2	6	11	14	15
5	13	17	39	46	47	49	1	2	4	7	13	22
6	22	26	38	39	41	42	1	[1]	2	4	12	29
7	06	18	40	43	47	49	2	3	4	6	12	22
8	05	18	26	34	42	49	5	[7]	[8]	8	8	[13]
9	01	05	11	19	28	36	4	6	8	8	9	14
10	01	09	16	34	38	41	3	4	7	8	9	18
11	01	09	14	20	43	44	1	5	6	6	8	23
12	09	14	26	28	30	45	2	2	5	[12]	13	15
13	03	35	39	42	44	48	2	3	4	4	[4]	32
14	23	24	30	31	33	37	1	1	2	4	6	[35]
15	13	16	23	29	36	49	3	6	7	7	13	13
16	14	20	21	30	41	46	1	5	6	9	11	17
17	11	17	24	28	41	47	4	6	6	7	13	13
18	04	33	34	38	39	49	1	1	4	4	10	29
19	03	06	09	12	40	43	3	3	3	[3]	9	28
20	17	19	20	32	36	48	1	2	4	12	12	18
21	03	15	19	24	28	34	4	4	5	6	12	18
22	01	10	33	35	38	43	2	3	5	7	9	23
23	02	03	23	33	40	46	1	5	6	7	10	20
24	08	17	33	41	43	45	2	2	8	9	12	16
25	06	12	19	25	31	41	[6]	6	6	7	10	14
26	10	11	17	34	38	46	1	4	6	8	13	17
27	16	22	28	30	33	35	2	2	3	6	6	30
28	15	27	35	37	38	39	1	1	2	8	12	25
29	03	10	21	25	29	49	3	4	4	7	11	20
30	04	18	22	27	44	48	4	4	5	5	14	17
31	12	23	25	26	34	49	1	2	8	11	12	15
32	06	10	11	19	22	46	1	3	4	8	9	24
33	02	12	26	32	37	47	4	5	6	10	10	14
34	07	13	17	33	40	42	2	4	6	7	14	16
35	03	27	34	41	42	48	1	4	6	7	7	24
36	04	10	20	24	39	49	4	4	6	10	10	15
37	03	07	12	21	25	36	4	4	5	9	11	16
38	03	12	15	18	30	31	1	3	3	9	12	21
39	01	09	10	11	16	49	1	1	[1]	5	8	33
40	05	06	18	22	24	38	1	2	4	12	14	16
41	07	11	12	36	38	39	1	1	2	4	[17]	24
42	04	15	25	27	33	40	1	2	6	7	13	20
43	06	08	10	13	22	32	2	2	3	9	10	23
44	03	10	22	25	31	49	3	3	6	7	12	18
45	05	11	13	18	25	35	2	5	6	7	10	19
46	11	16	20	22	27	46	2	4	5	5	14	19
47	01	14	25	37	39	47	2	3	8	11	12	13
48	12	24	33	36	39	42	3	3	3	9	12	19
49	04	06	10	11	24	33	1	2	4	9	13	20
50	12	22	25	43	46	49	3	3	3	10	12	18
51	11	13	14	16	21	44	1	2	2	5	16	23
52	04	13	23	28	30	32	2	2	5	9	10	21

These differences were then placed in ascending order thus: 1, 4, 4, 6, 10, and 24. These numbers are listed in the first line of the analysis in Chart 37, then the rest of the chart was constructed using the rest of the 2007 U.K. lottery results. I then highlighted the lowest and highest difference in each of the columns:

In the first column, the lowest figure is 1 and the highest figure is 6. In the second column, the lowest is 1 and the highest is 7. In the third column, 1 and 8. In the fourth column, 3 and 12. In the fifth column, 4 and 17. In the sixth column, 13 and 35.

The above table can help us formulate yet another valuable policy to follow, but first we must go through the same procedures with the 2007 Canadian Lotto results to see if we can confirm the policy.

Have a look at Chart 38. Here, I dealt with the Canadian results in the same way I did the U.K. results in Chart 37. The lottery results were arranged in ascending order, the difference between each number was calculated, these differences were then arranged in ascending order, and then the highest and lowest differences were identified. These differences are summarized below:

In the first column, the lowest figure is 1 and the highest figure is 5. In the second column, the lowest is 1 and the highest is 7. In the third column, 2 and 9. In the fourth column, 3 and 12. In the fifth column, 7 and 16. In the sixth column, 10 and 30.

The above Canadian list is slightly different from the U.K. Lottery list. To ensure as safe as possible a policy, it is best to adopt the lowest number found in either chart and the highest number found in either chart. So, after you have calculated the differences between the numbers of your proposed line of future lottery numbers, arrange them in ascending order. Then:

- *Ensure that the difference between the first and second number is within the range of 1 to 5. (I always go for a difference of 1 or 2)*
- *Ensure that the difference between the second and third number is within the range of 1 and 7.*
- *Ensure that the difference between the third and fourth number is within the range of 1 and 9.*
- *Ensure that the difference between the forth and fifth number is within the range of 3 and 12.*
- *Ensure that the difference between the fifth and sixth number is within the range of 6 and 17.*
- *Ensure that the difference between the sixth and first number is within the range of 10 and 35.*

CHART 38

CANADIAN LOTTO RESULTS 2007
ANALYSIS OF THE DIFFERENCES BETWEEN LOTTERY NUMBERS DRAWN THEN PLACED IN ASCENDING ORDER

WEEK No.	LOTTERY NUMBERS						DIFFERENCES BETWEEN WHEN PLACED IN ASCENDING ORDER					
1	19	20	33	43	45	47	1	2	2	10	13	21
2	01	02	03	19	25	41	1	1	6	9	16	16
3	24	40	45	47	48	49	1	1	2	5	16	24
4	06	09	17	20	22	40	2	3	3	8	15	18
5	10	13	24	27	37	39	2	3	3	10	11	20
6	08	13	23	37	41	42	1	4	5	10	14	15
7	13	20	31	36	43	46	3	5	7	7	11	16
8	04	06	15	33	38	40	2	2	5	9	13	18
9	03	21	27	37	43	44	1	6	6	8	10	18
10	09	18	28	37	42	49	5	7	9	9	9	10
11	13	21	23	27	28	34	1	2	4	6	8	28
12	01	13	19	26	32	46	4	6	6	7	12	14
13	04	09	16	32	37	41	4	5	5	7	12	16
14	10	12	23	26	35	37	2	2	3	9	11	22
15	06	15	22	26	41	49	4	6	7	8	9	15
16	17	29	33	43	45	49	2	4	4	10	12	17
17	03	19	20	23	35	38	1	3	3	12	14	16
18	01	23	26	28	33	40	2	3	5	7	10	22
19	05	07	13	27	45	47	2	2	6	7	14	18
20	08	16	33	37	40	42	2	3	4	8	15	17
21	06	17	29	32	36	47	3	4	8	11	11	12
22	08	16	19	32	40	46	3	6	8	8	11	13
23	10	20	25	41	44	46	2	3	5	10	13	16
24	03	15	31	33	43	48	2	4	5	10	12	16
25	07	20	24	37	43	49	4	6	6	7	13	13
26	06	12	25	43	45	47	2	2	6	8	13	18
27	10	19	25	31	37	40	3	6	6	6	9	19
28	10	27	33	38	40	49	2	5	6	9	10	17
29	09	10	22	29	38	41	1	3	7	9	12	17
30	01	05	17	32	39	45	4	5	6	7	12	15
31	09	17	18	20	41	49	1	2	8	8	9	21
32	01	17	23	34	37	49	1	3	6	11	12	16
33	02	12	32	34	38	48	2	3	4	10	10	20
34	09	19	31	35	39	42	3	4	4	10	12	16
35	11	17	18	28	31	46	1	3	6	10	14	15
36	03	08	16	20	24	25	1	4	4	5	8	27
37	09	39	40	43	46	48	1	2	3	3	10	30
38	05	08	12	15	39	47	3	3	4	8	7	24
39	09	19	26	29	39	45	3	6	7	10	10	13
40	05	15	30	35	41	48	5	6	6	7	10	15
41	01	26	30	32	39	47	2	3	4	7	8	25
42	07	08	13	26	32	35	1	3	5	6	13	21
43	12	13	17	34	40	47	1	4	6	7	14	17
44	08	23	33	40	46	49	3	6	7	8	10	15
45	03	13	14	17	20	42	1	3	3	10	10	22
46	14	17	27	41	47	48	1	3	6	10	14	15
47	01	10	25	27	30	36	2	3	6	9	14	15
48	16	21	31	40	43	45	2	3	5	9	10	20
49	02	09	11	22	35	45	2	6	7	10	11	13
50	03	11	32	34	44	48	2	4	4	8	10	21
51	08	17	30	36	40	47	4	6	7	9	10	13
52	07	13	16	24	35	42	3	6	7	8	11	14

CHART 39

UK 2007 SATURDAY RESULTS
ANALYSIS OF 'SQUARED' LOTTERY NUMBERS

WEEK No.	LOTTERY NUMBERS DRAWN						TOTAL IN WEEK	NUMBER OF TIMES PER WEEK IN YEAR						
								0	1	2	3	4	5	6
1	15	25	29	35	39	40	1	X	X	X	X	X		
2	05	08	12	20	28	48	0	X	X	X	X			
3	04	07	26	28	39	49	2	X	X	X				
4	04	15	21	23	24	38	1	X	X	X				
5	13	17	39	46	47	49	1	X	X	X				
6	22	26	38	39	41	42	0	X	X	X				
7	06	18	40	43	47	49	1	X	X	X				
8	05	18	26	34	42	49	1	X	X	X				
9	01	05	11	19	28	36	2	X	X	X				
10	01	09	16	34	38	41	3	X	X	X				
11	01	09	14	20	43	44	2	X	X	X				
12	09	14	26	28	30	45	1	X	X	X				
13	03	35	39	42	44	48	0	X	X					
14	23	24	30	31	33	37	0	X	X					
15	13	16	23	29	36	49	3	X	X					
16	14	20	21	30	41	46	0	X	X					
17	11	17	24	28	41	47	0	X	X					
18	04	33	34	38	39	49	2	X	X					
19	03	06	09	12	40	43	1		X					
20	17	19	20	32	36	48	1	18	19	12	2	1	0	0
21	03	15	19	24	28	34	0							
22	01	10	33	35	38	43	1							
23	02	03	23	33	40	46	0							
24	08	17	33	41	43	45	0							
25	06	12	19	25	31	41	1							
26	10	11	17	34	38	46	0							
27	16	22	28	30	33	35	1							
28	15	27	35	37	38	39	0							
29	03	10	21	25	29	49	2							
30	04	18	22	27	44	48	1							
31	12	23	25	26	34	49	2							
32	06	10	11	19	22	46	0							
33	02	12	26	32	37	47	0							
34	07	13	17	33	40	42	0							
35	03	27	34	41	42	48	0							
36	04	10	20	24	39	49	2							
37	03	07	12	21	25	36	2							
38	03	12	15	18	30	31	0							
39	01	09	10	11	16	49	4							
40	05	06	18	22	24	38	0							
41	07	11	12	36	38	39	1							
42	04	15	25	27	33	40	2							
43	06	08	10	13	22	32	0							
44	03	10	22	25	31	49	2							
45	05	11	13	18	25	35	1							
46	11	16	20	22	27	46	1							
47	01	14	25	37	39	47	2							
48	12	24	33	36	39	42	1							
49	04	06	10	11	24	33	1							
50	12	22	25	43	46	49	2							
51	11	13	14	16	21	44	1							
52	04	13	23	28	30	32	1							

Chapter 22
Considering Squared Numbers

HAVE a look at Chart 39. This time, we are looking at the U.K. results in which I have analyzed the squared numbers. A squared number is derived from multiplying a number by itself. For example, the squared numbers that occur in the lottery range of numbers are:

> 1, derived from 1 x 1;
> 4, derived from 2 x 2;
> 9, derived from 3 x 3;
> 16, derived from 4 x 4;
> 25, derived from 5 x 5;
> 36, derived from 6 x 6;
> 49, derived from 7 x 7.

In eighteen weeks of 2007, there were no squared numbers present. In nineteen weeks of that year there was one squared number present. In twelve weeks of that year there were two squared numbers present. In two weeks of that year there were three squared numbers present. In one week of that year there were four squared numbers present. More to the point, in no weeks of that year were there five or six squared numbers present. Before we commit ourselves to a policy reflecting this fact, you know what we must do.

Have a look at Chart 40 *(next page)*, the results of the 2007 Canadian Lotto Chart analyzed for squared numbers. It is very similar to the U.K. chart, but there is a slight difference. There are not four squared numbers present in any one week. So, taking the approach of being safe in our policy making the policy should now be: *When choosing a line of future*

CHART 40

CANADIAN LOTTO RESULTS 2007
ANALYSIS OF 'SQUARED' LOTTERY NUMBERS

WEEK No.	LOTTERY NUMBERS DRAWN						TOTAL IN WEEK	0	1	2	3	4	5	6
1	19	20	33	43	45	47	0	X	X	X	X			
2	[01]	02	03	19	[25]	41	2	X	X	X	X			
3	24	40	45	47	48	[49]	1	X	X	X				
4	06	[09]	17	20	22	40	1	X	X	X				
5	10	13	24	27	37	39	0	X	X	X				
6	08	13	23	37	41	42	0	X	X					
7	13	20	31	[36]	43	46	1	X	X					
8	[04]	06	15	33	38	40	1	X	X					
9	03	21	27	37	43	44	0	X	X					
10	[09]	18	28	37	42	[49]	2	X	X					
11	13	21	23	27	28	34	0	X	X					
12	[01]	13	19	26	32	46	1	X	X					
13	[04]	[09]	[16]	32	37	41	3	X	X					
14	10	12	23	26	35	37	0	X	X					
15	06	15	22	26	41	[49]	1	X	X					
16	17	29	33	43	45	[49]	1	X	X					
17	03	19	20	23	35	38	0	X	X					
18	[01]	23	26	28	33	40	1	X	X					
19	05	07	13	27	45	47	0	X	X					
20	08	[16]	33	37	40	42	1		X					
21	06	17	29	32	[36]	47	0		X					
22	08	[16]	19	32	40	46	1		X					
23	10	20	[25]	41	44	46	1		X					
24	03	15	31	33	43	48	0		X					
25	07	20	24	37	43	[49]	1		X					
26	06	12	[25]	43	45	47	1		X					
27	10	19	[25]	31	37	40	1	19	26	5	2	0	0	0
28	10	27	33	38	40	[49]	1							
29	[09]	10	22	29	38	41	1							
30	[01]	05	17	32	39	45	1							
31	[09]	17	18	20	41	[49]	2							
32	[01]	17	23	34	37	[49]	2							
33	02	12	32	34	38	48	0							
34	[09]	19	31	35	39	42	1							
35	11	17	18	28	31	46	0							
36	03	08	[16]	20	24	[25]	2							
37	[09]	39	40	43	46	48	1							
38	05	08	12	15	39	47	0							
39	[09]	19	26	29	39	45	1							
40	05	15	30	35	41	48	0							
41	[01]	26	30	32	39	47	1							
42	07	08	13	26	32	35	0							
43	12	13	17	34	40	47	0							
44	08	23	33	40	46	[49]	1							
45	03	13	14	17	20	42	0							
46	14	17	27	41	47	48	0							
47	[01]	10	[25]	27	30	[36]	3							
48	[16]	21	31	40	43	45	1							
49	02	[09]	11	22	35	45	1							
50	03	11	32	34	44	48	0							
51	08	17	30	[36]	40	47	1							
52	07	13	[16]	24	35	42	1							

lottery numbers, ensure that five or six of them are not squared numbers.
For example: If you choose 1, 4, 13, 25, 36, and 41, this would not be acceptable as four of these numbers (1, 4, 25, and 36) are squared. Likewise,
if you choose 4, 9, 25, 36, 48, and 49, this would also be not acceptable as
five of them (4, 9, 25, 36, and 49) are squared numbers.

Chapter 23

Considering Fibonacci Numbers

IN Chart 41, we are examining 2007 U.K. Lottery numbers from the point of view of Fibonacci numbers. These numbers are derived from a sequence in which each number is the sum of its two predecessors.

For example:

$$1 + 1 = 2$$
$$2 + 1 = 3$$
$$3 + 2 = 5$$
$$5 + 3 = 8$$
$$8 + 5 = 13$$
$$13 + 8 = 21$$
$$21 + 13 = 34$$

The list consists of 1, 2, 3, 5, 8, 13, 21, and 34. (The next number would be 55, but this is outside our range.)

Out of the eight Fibonacci numbers available in our range of 1 through 49, there were never more than two drawn in any one week. This could be the making of another worthwhile policy but, of course, we must check with the Canadian Lotto chart before we decide.

Looking at the Canadian Lotto analyzed in Chart 42 *(next page)*, we see that there was never a week where there were four, five, or six Fibonacci numbers present. In the previous chart we observed that there was never a week where there were three, four, five, or six Fibonacci numbers represented. So, if we choose the safe option of allowing a possible show-

CHART 41

UK 2007 SATURDAY RESULTS
ANALYSIS OF 'FIBONACCI' LOTTERY NUMBERS

WEEK No.	LOTTERY NUMBERS DRAWN						TOTAL IN WEEK	NUMBER OF TIMES PER WEEK IN YEAR						
								0	1	2	3	4	5	6
1	15	25	29	35	39	40	0	X	X	X				
2	05	08	12	20	28	48	2	X	X	X				
3	04	07	26	28	39	49	0	X	X	X				
4	04	15	21	23	24	38	1	X	X	X				
5	13	17	39	46	47	49	1	X	X	X				
6	22	26	38	39	41	42	0	X	X	X				
7	06	18	40	43	47	49	0	X	X	X				
8	05	18	26	34	42	49	2	X	X	X				
9	01	05	11	19	28	36	2	X	X	X				
10	01	09	16	34	38	41	2	X	X	X				
11	01	09	14	20	43	44	1	X	X	X				
12	09	14	26	28	30	45	0	X	X	X				
13	03	35	39	42	44	48	0	X	X					
14	23	24	30	31	33	37	0	X	X					
15	13	16	23	29	36	49	1	X	X					
16	14	20	21	30	41	46	1	X	X					
17	11	17	24	28	41	47	0	X	X					
18	04	33	34	38	39	49	1	X	X					
19	03	06	09	12	40	43	1	X	X					
20	17	19	20	32	36	48	0	X						
21	03	15	19	24	28	34	2	X						
22	01	10	33	35	38	43	1	21	19	12	0	0	0	0
23	02	03	23	33	40	46	2							
24	08	17	33	41	43	45	1							
25	06	12	19	25	31	41	0							
26	10	11	17	34	38	46	1							
27	16	22	28	30	33	35	0							
28	15	27	35	37	38	39	0							
29	03	10	21	25	29	49	2							
30	04	18	22	27	44	48	0							
31	12	23	25	26	34	49	1							
32	06	10	11	19	22	46	0							
33	02	12	26	32	37	47	1							
34	07	13	17	33	40	42	1							
35	03	27	34	41	42	48	2							
36	04	10	20	24	39	49	0							
37	03	07	12	21	25	36	2							
38	03	12	15	18	30	31	1							
39	01	09	10	11	16	49	1							
40	05	06	18	22	24	38	1							
41	07	11	12	36	38	39	0							
42	04	15	25	27	33	40	0							
43	06	08	10	13	22	32	2							
44	03	10	22	25	31	49	1							
45	05	11	13	18	25	35	2							
46	11	16	20	22	27	46	0							
47	01	14	25	37	39	47	1							
48	12	24	33	36	39	42	0							
49	04	06	10	11	24	33	0							
50	12	22	25	43	46	49	0							
51	11	13	14	16	21	44	2							
52	04	13	23	28	30	32	1							

CHART 42

CANADIAN LOTTO RESULTS 2007
ANALYSIS OF 'FIBONACCI' LOTTERY NUMBERS

WEEK No.	LOTTERY NUMBERS DRAWN						TOTAL IN WEEK	NUMBER OF TIMES PER WEEK IN YEAR						
								0	1	2	3	4	5	6
1	19	20	33	43	45	47	0	X	X	X	X			
2	01	02	03	19	25	41	3	X	X	X	X			
3	24	40	45	47	48	49	0	X	X	X				
4	06	09	17	20	22	40	0	X	X	X				
5	10	13	24	27	37	39	1	X	X	X				
6	08	13	23	37	41	42	2	X	X	X				
7	13	20	31	36	43	46	1	X	X	X				
8	04	06	15	33	38	40	0	X	X	X				
9	03	21	27	37	43	44	2	X	X	X				
10	09	18	28	37	42	49	0	X	X	X				
11	13	21	23	27	28	34	3	X	X	X				
12	01	13	19	26	32	46	2	X	X	X				
13	04	09	16	32	37	41	0	X	X	X				
14	10	12	23	26	35	37	0	X	X					
15	06	15	22	26	41	49	0	X	X					
16	17	29	33	43	45	49	0	X						
17	03	19	20	23	35	38	1	X						
18	01	23	26	28	33	40	1	X						
19	05	07	13	27	45	47	2	X						
20	08	16	33	37	40	42	1	X						
21	06	17	29	32	36	47	0	X						
22	08	16	19	32	40	46	1	X						
23	10	20	25	41	44	46	0	22	15	13	2	0	0	0
24	03	15	31	33	43	48	1							
25	07	20	24	37	43	49	0							
26	06	12	25	43	45	47	0							
27	10	19	25	31	37	40	0							
28	10	27	33	38	40	49	0							
29	09	10	22	29	38	41	0							
30	01	05	17	32	39	45	2							
31	09	17	18	20	41	49	0							
32	01	17	23	34	37	49	2							
33	02	12	32	34	38	48	2							
34	09	19	31	35	39	42	0							
35	11	17	18	28	31	46	0							
36	03	08	16	20	24	25	2							
37	09	39	40	43	46	48	0							
38	05	08	12	15	39	47	2							
39	09	19	26	29	39	45	0							
40	05	15	30	35	41	48	1							
41	01	26	30	32	39	47	1							
42	07	08	13	26	32	35	2							
43	12	13	17	34	40	47	2							
44	08	23	33	40	46	49	1							
45	03	13	14	17	20	42	2							
46	14	17	27	41	47	48	0							
47	01	10	25	27	30	36	1							
48	16	21	31	40	43	45	1							
49	02	09	11	22	35	45	1							
50	03	11	32	34	44	48	2							
51	08	17	30	36	40	47	1							
52	07	13	16	24	35	42	1							

ing of three Fibonacci numbers to exist in our future selections, we can happily adopt a policy that says: *When choosing a line of future lottery numbers, ensure that four, five, or six of them are not Fibonacci numbers.*

Fibonacci within the lottery range

are 1, 2, 3, 5, 8, 13, 21, and 34.

If you happened to choose 4, 5, 13, 21, 33, and 34 as your future lottery numbers, that would not be acceptable as four of them (5, 13, 21, and 34) are Fibonacci numbers.

Chapter 24

Considering Lucas Numbers

HAVE a look at Chart 43. This time we are examining lottery results from the point of view of Lucas numbers. This sequence of numbers is made up by beginning with 1 and 3. You then proceed by adding each prior two numbers to create the next number in the sequence.

For example:

$$1 + 3 = 4$$
$$3 + 4 = 7$$
$$4 + 7 = 11$$
$$7 + 11 = 18$$
$$11 + 18 = 29$$
$$18 + 29 = 47$$

It is much like the Fibonacci series. The numbers in this sequence that occur within the lottery range are: 1, 3, 4, 7, 11, 18, 29, and 47. I'm sure you know the form by now. Looking at this chart, you will see that there was never a week where there were four, five, or six Lucas numbers present. As you know, that has the making of a policy. We could say that *when choosing a line of lottery numbers, we should ensure that there are never four, five, or six Lucas numbers present.*

However, we must now check with the Canadian Lotto numbers to see if we can safely adopt this policy.

Have a look at Chart 44 *(next page)*. As you can clearly see, this chart shows that there were no weeks in the year where there were three, four, five, or six Lucas numbers present. So, to be on the safe side, the logical conclusion we are drawn to is that *when choosing a line of future lottery*

CHART 43

UK 2007 SATURDAY RESULTS
ANALYSIS OF 'LUCAS' LOTTERY NUMBERS

WEEK No.	LOTTERY NUMBERS DRAWN						TOTAL IN WEEK	NUMBER OF TIMES PER WEEK IN YEAR						
								0	1	2	3	4	5	6
1	15	25	29	35	39	40	1	X	X	X	X			
2	05	08	12	20	28	48	0	X	X	X				
3	04	07	26	28	39	49	2	X	X	X				
4	04	15	21	23	24	38	1	X	X	X				
5	13	17	39	46	47	49	1	X	X	X				
6	22	26	38	39	41	42	0	X	X	X				
7	06	18	40	43	47	49	2	X	X	X				
8	05	18	26	34	42	49	1	X	X	X				
9	01	05	11	19	28	36	2	X	X	X				
10	01	09	16	34	38	41	1	X	X	X				
11	01	09	14	20	43	44	1	X	X	X				
12	09	14	26	28	30	45	0	X	X	X				
13	03	35	39	42	44	48	1	X	X					
14	23	24	30	31	33	37	0	X	X					
15	13	16	23	29	36	49	1		X					
16	14	20	21	30	41	46	0		X					
17	11	17	24	28	41	47	2		X					
18	04	33	34	38	39	49	1		X					
19	03	06	09	12	40	43	1		X					
20	17	19	20	32	36	48	0		X					
21	03	15	19	24	28	34	1		X					
22	01	10	33	35	38	43	1		X					
23	02	03	23	33	40	46	1		X					
24	08	17	33	41	43	45	0		X					
25	06	12	19	25	31	41	0		X					
26	10	11	17	34	38	46	1	14	25	12	1	0	0	0
27	16	22	28	30	33	35	0							
28	15	27	35	37	38	39	0							
29	03	10	21	25	29	49	2							
30	04	18	22	27	44	48	2							
31	12	23	25	26	34	49	0							
32	06	10	11	19	22	46	1							
33	02	12	26	32	37	47	1							
34	07	13	17	33	40	42	1							
35	03	27	34	41	42	48	1							
36	04	10	20	24	39	49	1							
37	03	07	12	21	25	36	2							
38	03	12	15	18	30	31	2							
39	01	09	10	11	16	49	2							
40	05	06	18	22	24	38	1							
41	07	11	12	36	38	39	2							
42	04	15	25	27	33	40	1							
43	06	08	10	13	22	32	0							
44	03	10	22	25	31	49	1							
45	05	11	13	18	25	35	3							
46	11	16	20	22	27	46	1							
47	01	14	25	37	39	47	2							
48	12	24	33	36	39	42	0							
49	04	06	10	11	24	33	2							
50	12	22	25	43	46	49	0							
51	11	13	14	16	21	44	1							
52	04	13	23	28	30	32	1							

CHART 44

CANADIAN LOTTO RESULTS 2007
ANALYSIS OF 'LUCAS' LOTTERY NUMBERS

WEEK No.	LOTTERY NUMBERS DRAWN						TOTAL IN WEEK	NUMBER OF TIMES PER WEEK IN YEAR						
								0	1	2	3	4	5	6
1	19	20	33	43	45	[47]	1	X	X	X				
2	[01]	02	[03]	19	25	41	2	X	X	X				
3	24	40	45	[47]	48	49	1	X	X	X				
4	06	09	17	20	22	40	0	X	X	X				
5	10	13	24	27	37	39	0	X	X	X				
6	08	13	23	37	41	42	0	X	X	X				
7	13	20	31	36	43	46	0	X	X					
8	[04]	06	15	33	38	40	1	X	X					
9	[03]	21	27	37	43	44	1	X	X					
10	09	[18]	28	37	42	49	1	X	X					
11	13	21	23	27	28	34	0	X	X					
12	[01]	13	19	26	32	46	1	X	X					
13	[04]	09	16	32	37	41	1	X	X					
14	10	12	23	26	35	37	0	X	X					
15	06	15	22	26	41	49	0	X	X					
16	17	[29]	33	43	45	49	1	X	X					
17	03	19	20	23	35	38	0	X	X					
18	[01]	23	26	28	33	40	1	X	X					
19	05	[07]	13	27	45	[47]	2	X	X					
20	08	16	33	37	40	42	0		X					
21	06	17	[29]	32	36	[47]	2		X					
22	08	16	19	32	40	46	0		X					
23	10	20	25	41	44	46	0		X					
24	[03]	15	31	33	43	48	1		X					
25	[07]	20	24	37	43	49	1		X					
26	06	12	25	43	45	[47]	1		X					
27	10	19	25	31	37	40	0		X					
28	10	27	33	38	40	49	0	19	27	6	0	0	0	0
29	09	10	22	[29]	38	41	1							
30	[01]	05	17	32	39	45	1							
31	09	17	[18]	20	41	49	1							
32	[01]	17	23	34	37	49	1							
33	02	12	32	34	38	48	0							
34	09	19	31	35	39	42	0							
35	[11]	17	[18]	28	31	46	2							
36	[03]	08	16	20	24	25	1							
37	09	39	40	43	46	48	0							
38	05	08	12	15	39	[47]	1							
39	09	19	26	[29]	39	45	1							
40	05	15	30	35	41	48	0							
41	[01]	26	30	32	39	[47]	2							
42	[07]	08	13	26	32	35	1							
43	12	13	17	34	40	[47]	1							
44	08	23	33	40	46	49	0							
45	[03]	13	14	17	20	42	1							
46	14	17	27	41	[47]	48	1							
47	[01]	10	25	27	30	36	1							
48	16	21	31	40	43	45	0							
49	02	09	[11]	22	35	45	1							
50	[03]	[11]	32	34	44	48	2							
51	08	17	30	36	40	[47]	1							
52	[07]	13	16	24	35	42	1							

numbers, ensure that there are never four, five, or six Lucas numbers present. If you happen to choose 4, 5, 11, 18, 29, and 47 as your line of future lottery numbers, that would be unacceptable as five of them (4, 11, 18, 29, and 47) are Lucas numbers.

Lucas numbers within lottery range

are 1, 3, 4, 7, 11, 18, 29, and 47.

Chapter 25

I Could Go On...

THERE are many other sets of numbers that we could analyse. Not all of them are as obvious as the ones used in this book. To be honest, the Fibonacci and Lucas series were getting close to being in the realm of an order/chaos description. There are literally scores of number sequences that can be represented by a polynomial formula. Their sequences are so complicated that they can not be considered ordered. Therefore, there is no value in analyzing them. So, we have reached the end of our analysis.

Remember, you can purchase my Randomness Checking Program for Lottery Numbers at www.lotteryhelp.com. It is obtainable in six from forty-nine numbers, six from fifty numbers, six from fifty-four numbers, and six from fifty-nine numbers. It does all the checking for you in a fraction of a second! It even has the facility to choose *and check* a set of numbers for you.

Thank you for bearing with me thus far. If you wish to contact me on a numerical matter, I would be happy for you to do so. Please route your queries to me at the address page toward the end of the book.

Good hunting!

Harry Schneider
June 2008

Chapter 26

In Summary

REMEMBER, when choosing a line of your future lottery numbers you should ensure that:

they are not either all odd or all even;
five or six of them are not exactly divisible by 3;
five or six of them are not exactly divisible by 4;
five or six of them are not exactly divisible by 5;
four, five, or six of them are not exactly divisible by 6;
four, five, or six of them are not exactly divisible by 7;
four, five, or six of them are not exactly divisible by 8;
three, four, or five of them are not exactly divisible by 9;
three or four of them are not exactly divisible by 10;
three or four of them are not exactly divisible by 11;
three or four of them are not exactly divisible by 12;
three of them are not exactly divisible by 13;
three of them are not exactly divisible by 14;
three of them are not exactly divisible by 15;
three of them are not exactly divisible by 16;
four, five, or six of them are not in the units series;
five or six of them are not in the tens series;
five or six of them are not in the twenties series;
five or six of them are not in the thirties series;
five or six of them are not in the forties series;
five or six of them are not in the prime series;
there are never four or five of them ending in 1;

there are never four or five of them ending in 2;
there are never four or five of them ending in 3;
that there are never four or five of them ending in 4;
there are never four or five of them ending in 5;
there are never four or five of them ending in 6;
there are never four or five of them ending in 7;
there are never four or five of them ending in 8;
there are never four or five of them ending in 9;
when you add them together they never total less than 82 or more than 253;
the standard deviation value of the set is never less than 5 or more than 20;
the first number is within the range of 1 through 24;
the second number is within the range of 2 through 40;
the third number is within the range of 3 through 45;
the fourth number is within the range of 12 through 47;
the fifth number is within the range of 14 through 48; and
the sixth number is within the range of 25 through 49.

After the differences between the numbers have been calculated and arranged in ascending order, then ensure that:

the difference between the first and second number is within the range of 1 through 5;
the difference between the second and third number is within the range of 1 through 7;
the difference between the third and fourth number is within the range of 1 through 9;
the difference between the fourth and fifth number is within the range of 3 through 12;
the difference between the fifth and sixth number is within the range of 6 through 17;
the difference between the sixth and first number is within the range of 10 through 31;
five or six of them are not squared numbers;
four, five, or six of them are not in the Fibonacci series;
four, five, or six of them are not in the Lucas series.

Remember to adjust your selections to include the advice given on page 40.

Chapter 27

Three Ways to Play

NOW that you have plowed your way through these pages, you are now in a position to make full use of the benefits that ought to be clear to you. There are basically three ways to play the lottery:

- One way to play is to place one or two lines by yourself whenever you want, bearing in mind to check the validity of your selections as per the advice in this book. While I believe you now have an increased chance of some sort of win, the odds of winning a large sum are still very high. If you're serious in gaming with the lottery, you should consider staking as much as you can afford to lose without caring for any loss. This may put you in the category of the next sort of gamer.

- Another way to play is to create a small syndicate. This must be done on a formal basis with strict rules, etc. Your local lottery company will give you free advice as to how to proceed. Each member of the syndicate should be supplied with a copy of a Syndicate Agreement. With this small syndicate you might consider placing about eight lines weekly or multiples of eight. My advice is to cover as many numbers as possible.

- A third way to play is to create a large syndicate at your place of employment, a club, within your family, from your community, etc. Mathematically, the minimum size of play in this category would consist of forty-nine lines. This plan ensures that each number is covered exactly the same number of times (six). It's also a good idea to check each line through the Schneider Software Randomness Checking Program. This plan ensures that the first number drawn is featured in six lines. This plan is available from my web site at www.lotteryhelp.com.

Before using these plans, you should check how your own staking has fared over the past few months. This will put you in a position to compare your success rate with any plan acquired from Schneider Software. Remember to ensure that each member of your syndicate, including yourself, does not invest more than they are prepared to lose! This is most important!

Order Form

To use this form, simply enter your requirements and mail to the address below containing your check or postal money order. In order to retain the integrity of this book you could photocopy this page instead of cutting it out.

Please allow fourteen days for delivery.

Schneider Software
Rowan Bank, Wigtown Road, Sorbie
Newton Stewart
DG8 8EL SCOTLAND

Name _____

Address _____

_____

County/State _____

Country _____ Post Code/Zip _____

E-Mail _____

ITEM	Quantity	Cost Each	Total Cost
Randomness Checker (6/49)		£20/$40	
Randomness Checker (6/50)		£20/$40	
Randomness Checker (6/54)		£20/$40	
Randomness Checker (6/59)		£20/$40	
SCHNEIDER SOFTWARE 49 LINE PLAN		£10/$20	
TOTAL DUE: (50% Discount on subsequent purchases)			

Delivery options: ❏ email ❏ surface mail
You can also order direct from: www.lotteryhelp.com

LaVergne, TN USA
12 November 2009

163760LV00007B/2/P